First Impressions: Unforgettable Openings for Youth Meetings

Group
Loveland, Colorado

■ ■

First Impressions: Unforgettable Openings for Youth Meetings
Copyright © 1998 Group Publishing, Inc.

Credits
Compilation Editor: Pamela J. Shoup
Editor: Janis Sampson
Development Editor: Jody Brolsma
Chief Creative Officer: Joani Schultz
Copy Editor: Debbie Gowensmith
Art Director: Kari K. Monson
Cover Art Director: Jeff A. Storm
Designer: Lisa Chandler
Computer Graphic Artist: Nighthawk Design
Cover Photographers: Telegraph Colour Library/FPG International and Craig DeMartino
Cover Photo Illustrator: Randy Miller
Illustrator: Leslie Dunlap
Production Manager: Gingar Kunkel

Library of Congress Cataloging-in-Publication Data
First impressions : unforgettable openings for youth meetings.
  p. cm.
  Includes index.
  ISBN 0-7644-2000-3
  1. Church group work with youth. 2. Teenagers--Religious life.
I. Group Publishing.
BV4447.F58 1998
259'.23--dc21   97-53048
                   CIP

#38139494

10 9 8 7 6 5 4 3 2 1   07 06 05 04 03 02 01 00 99 98

Printed in the United States of America.

Table of Contents

Action Openings

Devotional Openings

Discussion-Starter Openings

Getting-to-Know-You Openings

Youth-Issue Openings

Special-Occasion Openings

Just-for-Fun Openings

Introduction

How do you open your youth meetings? Do you begin with a hymn? a generic prayer? or a "Sit down and be quiet"? Or maybe you just start talking to your students without a specific goal in mind and then drone on and on...ZZZ!

If you open your youth meeting in a way that captures teenagers' attention, you'll have their attention throughout the meeting. Get them excited about being together for lively discussions and Scripture studies.

With *First Impressions: Unforgettable Openings for Youth Meetings,* you have 115 tried-and-true openings for youth meetings. The activities in this book were written and tested by youth leaders like you and have appeared in GROUP Magazine and in books and curriculum published by Group Publishing.

Here are openings for any type of activity you might have planned for your group. Turn to "Action Openings" to get kids up on their feet and moving around. Let kids work off some of that excess energy as race-car teams, detectives, and bodybuilders.

For a more contemplative time together, try "Devotional Openings" to help your teenagers explore the power of prayer, trusting God, and God's blessings in their lives.

"Discussion-Starter Openings" will get your kids sharing their opinions and beliefs about such topics as faith, the Bible, sharing faith, and temptation. The discussion-starter questions will challenge kids to think about and analyze their opinions.

In your group, do you have new kids—or kids who want to get to know each other better? Turn to "Getting-to-Know-You Openings," and help kids learn one another's names, make new friends, and understand how to encourage one another.

"Youth-Issue Openings" explore a variety of topics of interest to your teens—peer pressure, parents, gossip, gangs, and AIDS, for example.

For those special seasons of the year, you'll find "Special-Occasion Openings," which focus on seasonal themes such as Christmas, Easter, and Valentine's Day.

And sometimes your teenagers just need to have some fun. That's why we've included "Just-for-Fun Openings"—games and activities with no particular theme except having a good time together.

We know how busy you are, so there's little or no preparation time involved in these meeting openings. And most openings require only simple supplies that are easy to find. We've also included a Scripture index for your convenience so you can easily tie an opening into a planned lesson or theme.

Start using *First Impressions: Unforgettable Openings for Youth Meetings* now to make a great first impression!

Action Openings

"Let the sea resound, and everything in it,
the world, and all who live in it. Let the rivers
clap their hands, let the mountains sing
together for joy; let them sing before the Lord."
PSALM 98:7-9a

*T*here's no better way to make a youth meeting lively than with an action opening! Get your teenagers excited about what's coming by getting them up on their feet to let off some steam. Teach them that praise can be lively and fun!

• Balloon Bump-Up •

PURPOSE: *to play a fast-paced game leading into a discussion on balancing priorities*

SCRIPTURE: *Ecclesiastes 3:1-8*

SUPPLIES: *balloons, markers, and a trash bag*

Have each teenager inflate and tie off a balloon. Collect all the balloons in a large trash bag, and have kids form two equal teams. Explain that team members must work together to keep every balloon in the air. Toss up a balloon for the first team; then after ten seconds, toss up another balloon. Continue tossing up a balloon every ten seconds until one hits the ground. Then do the same for the second team, and see which team successfully balances the most balloons.

After the game, give a balloon and a marker to each person. Have kids write on their balloons the activities and responsibilities they have to juggle every day. Then have each person bat his or her balloon in the air for several seconds. Call time, and have everyone sit on his or her balloon.

Encourage teenagers to discuss how they can balance school, home, and other activities, and also have time for God. Include a prayer asking God to help "burst" your students' busyness and help them prioritize their daily activities.

• Pick-a-Name Relay •

PURPOSE: *to creatively choose groups for any activity*

SCRIPTURE: *none*

SUPPLIES: *slips of paper, pencils, and a bowl or a paper sack*

This is a good getting-acquainted game and is a good way for kids to form groups for a Bible study or another activity. You'll need a large area—indoors or outdoors—for this activity.

Have each person write his or her name on a slip of paper. Place the slips of paper into the bowl. Draw out a number of slips equal to the number of groups you want to form. Read the names you've drawn, and designate those people as group leaders who will start the relay.

■ ■

Have everyone line up on a starting line twenty to thirty yards away from the bowl of names. Tell group leaders how many members they will need to gather during the relay. On "go," have each group leader run to the bowl, pick out a name slip, and run back to grab the hand of the person whose name is on the slip. Then have these two people run hand in hand back to the bowl, pick a name, and run back to grab the next person's hand. Have kids continue this process until each group has the correct number of members.

▪ Giant-slayers ▪

PURPOSE: *to understand that they need God's help to conquer problems*

SCRIPTURE: *1 Samuel 17*

SUPPLIES: *a Bible, newsprint, black markers, pens, and tape*

Before the meeting, draw a ceiling-tall outline of a giant on newsprint (the higher the ceiling, the better). If you have time, add a mean face, armor, and weapons to your giant drawing.

Securely tape the newsprint to a wall. Have kids line up single file a few feet away from the newsprint. Distribute black markers, and tell kids that to defeat the giant, someone must make a mark on the giant's forehead. Be sure kids keep their markers in their hands instead of throwing them. Let kids take turns jumping and making marks as high as possible on the giant. After everyone has had a turn, have kids stand on sturdy chairs to write their names by their marks. Ask:

● **Why was it hard to defeat the giant?**

Tell the story of David and Goliath in an exciting and dynamic way, using your Bible as a reference (1 Samuel 17). When you're finished, ask:

● **How is the way you tried to defeat the giant like the way David defeated Goliath? How is it different?**

● **In what ways did fighting Goliath help David rely on God?**

● **Why were the other Israelites afraid to depend on God's strength?**

● **What are some "giants" in your life right now?**

Give each person a pen, and have everyone write on the giant a description of one giant he or she is facing in life. For example, kids may write, "My best friend's mad at me" or "I got a D in English class" or "I'm sad because my dog died." When everyone is finished, have volunteers pray, thanking God for his help in "slaying giants" in their lives. Then let kids tear the giant down.

You can continue your meeting with further discussion of kids' personal problems; God's ability to help conquer problems; or a Christian perspective on world problems such as hunger, homelessness, and poverty.

· Sit Statements ·

PURPOSE: *to examine how they relate to their parents*

SCRIPTURE: *Proverbs 3; Ephesians 6:1-3; and Hebrews 12:7-11*

SUPPLIES: *a Bible*

Have teenagers sit in chairs in a circle. Say: **I'm going to read statements that may or may not reflect things that happened with your parents during the past week. If a statement is true for you, move in the direction I indicate. If it's not true for you, stay seated. If someone is in the seat you're supposed to move to, sit on that person's lap.**

Read aloud these "sit statements":

● **Move one seat to your right if you said, "I love you" to your parents.**

● **Move two seats to your left if you had an argument with your parents.**

● **Move one seat to your left if you fought with your parents about music.**

● **Move one seat to your left if your parents told you to clean your room.**

● **Move three seats to your left if you helped wash dishes.**

● **Move eight seats to your left if you were grounded.**

● **Move one seat to your right if you yelled at your parents.**

● **Move two seats to your right if you talked about school problems with your parents.**

● **Move five seats to your left if you spent time talking with your parents.**

● **Move one seat to your right if you helped cook a meal.**

After you've read the last statement, have kids return to their original seats. Ask:

● **What did you learn about the way you relate to your parents?**

■■

● Do you think you generally have a good or bad relationship with your parents? Explain.

Read aloud Ephesians 6:1-3, and then ask:

● Does this passage describe what goes on at your home? Why or why not?

● What can you do to make your home life reflect this passage?

Encourage students' feedback through your acceptance and understanding about their behavior toward parents. Treat gently those who find the discussion uncomfortable. Proverbs 3 and Hebrews 12:7-11 may also provide kids with helpful guidelines as they seek to welcome instruction from parents and discipline from God.

▪ In the Dark ▪

PURPOSE: *to think about heaven and hell*

SCRIPTURE: *Genesis 28:10-17; Nehemiah 9:6; Isaiah 66:1; Matthew 6:20-21; 10:28; Luke 12:5; 16:19-31; 2 Peter 2:4-22; and Revelation 15:5-8*

SUPPLIES: *blindfolds*

Say: **Today we're going to talk about places none of us has ever been—heaven and hell. When we think about these two places, we may feel as if we're just stumbling in the dark with unanswered questions. Let's play a game to experience those feelings.**

Instruct kids to stand in the middle of the room, and have them put on blindfolds. Say: **When I say "go," try to touch each wall of the room. Move slowly and carefully since everyone is doing this activity together. Ready? Go!**

Afterward, ask:

● How did you feel during this activity?

● How is that like feelings you have about heaven and hell?

Say: **Sometimes we may feel as if we're wandering in the dark when we think about heaven and hell. We've never been there, and we don't know anyone who has—except Jesus. But the Bible tells us about both of these places.**

You might continue with a study that explores what the Bible says about heaven and hell, using Scriptures such as Genesis 28:10-17; Nehemiah 9:6; Matthew 6:20-21; 10:28; Luke 12:5; 16:19-31; 2 Peter 2:4-22; and Revelation 15:5-8.

▪ How to Get Rich ▪

PURPOSE: *to play a game and compare the riches of the world to the riches offered by God*

SCRIPTURE: *Isaiah 55:1-9*

SUPPLIES: *a Bible, play money from page 15, tape, and a cake with a happy face on the top*

Before the meeting, decorate the room with play money. Tape the money under chairs; behind pictures; and on the ceiling, floor, and walls. The money should cover the room. Set the cake with the happy face in a prominent place in the room.

After the kids arrive, point out the money scattered around the room and the cake with the happy face. Then say: **You're going to play a game in which the goal is to collect as much money as possible in two minutes. Whoever collects the most money can buy this cake. You can steal money from others, but torn bills will not be counted. Ready? Go.**

After two minutes, shout "stop," and have kids sit down to count their money. Declare a winner, take his or her money, and give him or her the cake. Have kids form a circle, and ask the winner:

- **How did you feel when you won?**
- **Did winning make you happy? Why or why not?**

Ask everyone:

- **What was it like when you were scrambling to collect the money?**
- **How did you feel when someone tried to take your money?**
- **Were you disappointed that you didn't win? Why or why not?**
- **What's bad about the way we acted in this game?**
- **How is this game similar to our society? different from our society?**

Read aloud Isaiah 55:1-9. Ask:

- **What rewards do the rich enjoy? the poor?**
- **Do you think money can buy happiness? Explain.**
- **What are some "riches" money can't buy?**
- **How are God's riches different from the world's riches?**
- **How can we gain God's riches this week?**

■ Very Important People, Places, and Things ■

PURPOSE: *to learn more about the Bible*

SCRIPTURE: *various*

SUPPLIES: *Bibles, index cards, a pen, and tape*

Before the meeting, write on separate index cards the Scripture references and names of famous biblical people, places, and things. For example, for famous people you might write, "Samson—Judges 16," "Pontius Pilate—Matthew 27:11-26," and "Simon Peter—Mark 8:27-29; 14:66-72; John 21:15-19." Famous places could be the "Red Sea—Exodus 14:10-31," "Bethlehem—Luke 2:1-7," or "Jesus' tomb—John 19:38-20:9." Famous things could be "manna—Exodus 16:1-5," "Gideon's fleece—Judges 6:36-40," and "the cross—Matthew 27:27-37; Colossians 2:13-15." Write on one index card for each person.

As the kids arrive, tape an index card to each person's back. Tell kids that these cards are their name tags and that they must figure out who, where, or what they are. Tell group members to use Bibles and to ask each other yes-or-no questions to figure out what's written on the cards.

For example, someone might ask, "Am I a person? a place? a thing?" "Did I build the ark?" or "Did I lead the Israelites across the Red Sea?" Be sure kids don't tell each other what the index cards say—they may only answer "yes" or "no." The game is over when everyone discovers what's written on his or her card. Use this game to lead into a discussion on Bible reading or to begin a study on any particular Bible story used in the game.

■ The Prize ■

PURPOSE: *to learn that Jesus is the way to God*

SCRIPTURE: *John 14:6*

SUPPLIES: *a Bible, masking tape, gift wrap, scissors, tape, and a box*

Before your meeting, clear chairs, tables, and other obstacles from the center of the room. Place a chair against one wall where space has been cleared. Place two- to three-inch strips of masking tape in a random pattern on the floor. Kids will be stepping from strip to strip from various points in the room, heading toward the chair, so arrange tape strips so that some are close together while others require a bit of a jump for kids to reach them. Don't place any tape strips within five feet of the chair.

Gift-wrap a Bible, and place it on the chair. You may want to put the Bible in a box before wrapping it so it won't be obvious what the package contains.

When kids arrive, say: **The person who can figure out how to reach the prize while always stepping on a piece of tape wins the prize.**

Let kids attempt to reach the prize one at a time. (If your group is large, have several kids move about the area at one time.) Don't allow them to pick up and move pieces of tape. After everyone has tried, acknowledge kids' efforts but declare no winner.

In the area where there's no tape, add one long piece of tape reaching to the prize. Then have a volunteer step on the tape pieces to reach the prize. Have that person open the present and read aloud John 14:6 to the group. Ask:

● **The only way to reach the prize was with a bridge. How is Jesus like a bridge to God?**

● **How do people today try to reach God? Why do these ways fail?**

● **How does Jesus tell us to show our love for him?**

Have each person talk about one way he or she can be obedient to Jesus' teaching in the next week.

• Faith Building •

PURPOSE: *to explore the role of perseverance in faith*

SCRIPTURE: *James 1:2-4*

SUPPLIES: *a Bible and a fitness or muscle magazine*

Hold up a picture of a bodybuilder on the cover of a fitness or muscle magazine. Say: **Let's see if we can look like this body-builder.**

Lead everyone in exercises such as push-ups, sit-ups, and jumping jacks for at least five minutes. Then have kids form groups of no more than four. Have groups discuss the following questions:

● How many of you now look like the bodybuilder?

● How long does it take to develop muscles like those on our magazine cover?

● What is the role of perseverance in bodybuilding?

Ask someone to read aloud James 1:2-4. Ask:

● How are difficult situations like exercise?

● In what ways does relying on God build our faith?

● What spiritual muscles grow when we face trials?

● What is the role of perseverance in building your spiritual muscles?

Say: We may never look like the person on the cover of this magazine, but with perseverance and desire we can build spiritual muscles that will help us face any difficult situation.

■ Shoe Search ■

PURPOSE: *to learn the importance of effectively sharing the gospel with others*

SCRIPTURE: *Matthew 16:13-16; 28:16-20; Acts 1:6-8; 2 Timothy 3:14-4:5; and 1 Peter 3:13-17*

SUPPLIES: *a Bible*

Have kids remove their shoes and mix them up in a pile at one end of the room. Then have kids form teams of three or more at the opposite end of the room. Tell kids that the first person on each team is the "detective." Explain that the second person on each team will describe his or her shoes to the detective, who will run to find them in the shoe pile and bring them back.

If the detective brings back the wrong shoes, he or she must gather more clues and search again. If the detective brings back the right shoes, the owner will put them on and become the detective. Have kids repeat the process until one team finds all its shoes.

After the game, ask:

● What was difficult about this game?

● What was it like to describe your shoes to someone who didn't know what they looked like?

Read aloud 1 Peter 3:13-17. Ask:

● How is describing your shoes to a friend similar to presenting the gospel to your friends?

● What might happen if we don't present the gospel clearly?

● How can we become more effective at sharing Christ with others?

Continue with a discussion about clearly presenting the gospel of Jesus to those who are searching. Use Scriptures such as Matthew 16:13-16; 28:16-20; Acts 1:6-8; and 2 Timothy 3:14-4:5.

▪ Run to Win ▪

PURPOSE: *to learn what it means to run the race of life*

SCRIPTURE: *1 Corinthians 9:24-27*

SUPPLIES: *Bibles, a plain flag or piece of cloth, and masking tape*

Before class, use masking tape to mark the starting and finish lines in your room.

When kids arrive, have them form Race-Car Teams of five or Motorcycle Teams of three. Have kids line up on the starting line with their teams.

Say: **Each team represents an Indy-style race car** (or a motocross motorcycle). **One of you will be the "chassis," or framework, and the others will be the "wheels." The wheels must pick up and carry the chassis.**

When I shout, "Racers, start your engines!" the chassis should make roaring-engine noises. Then when I drop my flag, your race car will race along the outside edge of the room. The first race car to make five laps around the track wins. Ready? Racers, start your engines! Pause, and then quickly lower your flag.

When the race is finished, have kids sit together with their teams. Give each team a Bible. Ask a volunteer from each team to read aloud 1 Corinthians 9:24-27, and then have each team discuss these questions:

● **Did your team run to get a prize? Why or why not?**
● **What prize is Paul talking about?**
● **What are you doing to get the prize Paul's talking about?**

▪ Tearing Down ▪

PURPOSE: *to explore prejudice and overcoming differences*

SCRIPTURE: *John 4:5-26*

SUPPLIES: *Bibles, cards from the "Breaking In" handout (p. 21), pencils, and slips of paper*

As kids arrive, have each person pick from your hand one of the cards from the "Breaking In" handout. Tell kids to treat the information on their cards as top-secret.

Recruit two volunteers to make a mini-circle by holding hands. Show volunteers "Breaking-In Card #1," and instruct them to resist anyone who does not follow the exact directions on the card.

Welcome kids to the meeting. Say: **Your first assignment is to join the mini-circle formed by our two volunteers. And the only way you can join the circle is by following the directions on the card you chose. Once you're in the circle, don't allow anyone in the circle who doesn't follow the directions printed on your card.**

One at a time, have kids try to join the circle by following the directions on their cards. After all the kids have tried to join the mini-circle, gather everyone into a large group. Give each person a pencil and a slip of paper. Ask:

● How did it feel when you weren't allowed to join the circle?
● What was your attitude toward those in the circle?
● How did it feel if you did join the circle?
● What was your attitude toward those outside the circle?
● Was this game fair to everyone? Why or why not?

Ask for volunteers to read aloud John 4:5-26. Say: **The Samaritan woman probably felt a lot like those of you who couldn't break into the circle. The Jews refused to associate with Samaritans even though the Samaritans had no control over their ethnic background. In many ways today, we're no different from the people of biblical times. We avoid people just because they're different from us.**

Spend a minute thinking about one trait you don't like in others. For example, maybe you don't like people who make straight A's, or maybe you make fun of people who aren't good in sports. Write that one trait on your paper. No one will see your paper but you.

After one minute, ask:

● **Jesus was a Jew. Why do you think he talked to the Samaritan woman rather than avoid her as other Jews did?**
● **Why should you reach out to the people described on your cards?**

Use this activity to lead kids into a discussion on prejudice, stereotyping, and acceptance of others.

Breaking-In Card #1

1. Choose a spot to break into the circle.

2. Whisper, "God is great" into the ear of the person on the right of the spot you've chosen.

3. Whisper, "God is good" into the ear of the person on the left of the spot you've chosen.

4. Shout, "Amen!" as you try to break into the circle.

✂ -

Breaking-In Card #2

1. Choose a spot to break into the circle.

2. Whisper, "Let us thank God" into the ear of the person on the right of the spot you've chosen.

3. Whisper, "For our food" into the ear of the person on the left of the spot you've chosen.

4. Shout, "Amen!" as you try to break into the circle.

• Name That Sin •

PURPOSE: *to hold a "sin" race to learn about forgiveness*

SCRIPTURE: *John 3:16-17 and 1 John 1:5–2:2*

SUPPLIES: *newsprint, tape, and a marker*

Before class, tape a sheet of newsprint to a wall.

Have teenagers line up across the room from the newsprint. Give the first person a marker. Tell kids that when you say "go," the first person will run to the newsprint, write down a sin, run back to the line, and hand the marker to the next person. Then that person must run to the newsprint and write a different sin, and so on. Kids can help each other think of sins.

Say: **Go,** and then have kids run the relay for two minutes. Call time, and count the sins. Read the list aloud, and ask:

● **Was it easy or difficult to think of so many sins?**

● **Does God forgive all these sins? Why or why not?**

Ask kids to gather by the list. Give them one minute to rank the sins, with the number one sin as the worst sin. Then ask:

● **How did you decide which sin was worse than the others?**

● **How does God rank sin? Does he think one sin is worse than another? Explain.**

Say: **God doesn't want us to sin—and that means in any way. But God loves us so much—even though we're sinners—that he sent his Son to die for us. Jesus' death gives each of us the opportunity for true forgiveness. Let's discover more about sin and forgiveness.**

• An Eye for an Eye •

PURPOSE: *to discover biblical responses to violent behavior*

SCRIPTURE: *Matthew 5:38-42; Ephesians 6:10-18; James 4:7*

SUPPLIES: *a Bible and marshmallows*

Have kids form two teams, and have teams move to opposite sides of the room. Designate one team as the Cartoon Team and the other team as the Real-People Team. Give each team a supply of marshmallows.

Say: **Your goal is to get your opponents "out" by hitting them with marshmallows. You must stay on your side of the room. When you're out, you must lie still on the floor.**

Further explain that kids on the Real-People Team are out when they're each hit once by a marshmallow, but kids on the Cartoon Team aren't out until they're each hit five times.

Let kids play until one team is out. Ask:

● **Was this a fair fight? Why or why not?**

● **Is there really a winner when fighting or violence occurs? Why or why not?**

Have everyone stand on one side of the room. Then stand by yourself on the other side of the room. Say: **We're going to play the marshmallow game again, but this time you'll be one team, and I'll be the other team by myself. It'll take ten marshmallows to get me out, but only one to get any of you out.**

On "go," simply stand in place without throwing any marshmallows. When you've been hit ten times, fall to the ground, and pause for a minute.

Get back on your feet, and then read aloud Matthew 5:38-42. Ask:

● **How did you feel when I didn't fight back?**

● **What does this passage say about returning violence for violence?**

● **Do you agree with this passage? Why or why not?**

● **Is it always wrong to fight back? Why or why not?**

Lead kids into a brainstorming session and discussion on practical responses to violence and retaliation. For further study encourage kids to read about the armor of God in Ephesians 6:10-18 and submission to God in James 4:7.

▪ All You Need ▪

PURPOSE: *to understand that God is all they need*

SCRIPTURE: *Philippians 4:19*

SUPPLIES: *a Bible and a soft object to throw, such as a foam ball or a wadded-up pair of socks*

Have kids stand or sit in a circle. Say: **Let's play a game called All You Need. I'll begin with a statement and will throw the ball to someone in the circle. Whoever catches the ball will finish the statement. For example, if I say, "All you need to make spaghetti is..." and then throw the ball to you, you might say, "boiling water." And then you throw the ball to someone else, who might** say "meatballs." Then that person throws the ball to someone else, and so on. I'll interrupt with new statements, so don't be concerned if you don't get to answer every statement. Let's make sure everyone gets a chance to throw the ball.

Begin the game by saying: **All you need for a good party is...** Then have each person finish the statement as he or she catches the ball. As the game continues, interject the following statements:

- **All you need to fix a flat tire is...**
- **All you need for a great concert is...**
- **All you need for a perfect weekend is...**
- **All you need to be popular is...**
- **All you need to make friends is...**
- **All you need for peace is...**
- **All you need to get to heaven is...**

When the game is finished, read aloud Philippians 4:19. Then ask:

- **What was easy about this game? What was difficult?**
- **Which statements took more thought? Why?**
- **Is God all we need? Why or why not?**

Close the activity in prayer by passing around the ball and having each person complete the following prayer: "Lord, you're all I need for..."

• Rules as Tools •

PURPOSE: *to explore personal obedience to God*

SCRIPTURE: *Colossians 3:23-24*

SUPPLIES: *Bibles*

Say: **Let's play a game similar to Simon Says. The leader quickly will give a series of instructions to obey. Instructions might include "Hop on your right foot three times" or "Do ten jumping jacks."**

Choose one person to lead the game. Tell the class it'll have to listen carefully to the leader's directions. If the leader begins a direction with his or her name, such as "Whitney says," the class should obey the directions. If the leader omits his or her name, the class shouldn't obey.

Anyone who obeys a direction not preceded by the leader's name is out of the game and must sit down until the game is finished.

Start the game, and allow kids to play a few rounds, choosing a new leader each time. After the game have kids form trios to discuss these questions:

● Why was it hard to follow the directions correctly each time?

● How was playing this game like following God's directions?

● What was it like to have to stop playing the game after you obeyed the wrong direction?

● How was being separated from the game like what happens when we don't obey God?

Have kids read Colossians 3:23-24 together and then discuss these questions:

● How do you feel when someone tells you to do something you don't want to do?

● Why is it easier to obey certain people?

● When is it hard to obey your teachers? your parents? God?

Have each person tell a partner one step he or she will take toward becoming more obedient to God this week.

■ Good Sports ■

PURPOSE: *to learn how to lose and win gracefully*

SCRIPTURE: *Proverbs 27:1-2 and Matthew 5:3-10*

SUPPLIES: *masking tape, tennis balls, three permanent markers of different colors, and a simple prize*

Ahead of time, ask tennis-playing friends for old tennis balls for this activity. Use masking tape to mark off a starting line and a finish line that are at least fifteen feet apart.

Have kids form three teams. Instruct teams to line up behind the starting line, and give each person a ball. Use a marker to mark each team's tennis balls with the team's own color.

Say: **The object of this game is for team members to roll the balls to the finish line and back using only their feet. The first person in each line will kick a tennis ball to the finish line *and* back. Then the second person will kick his or her tennis ball and the first person's ball to the finish line and back. The game will continue this way, so the last person on each team will kick all the team's tennis balls to the finish line and back. The first team to get back all its tennis balls will win a prize.**

After a winner has been determined, award that team the prize. Then have kids form groups of three that consist of a person from each team. Ask:

- **What was it like to be on the winning team? a losing team?**
- **What was your initial reaction when another team won?**
- **What were your feelings toward team members who had a tough time kicking the tennis balls?**

Say: **Winning and losing have become significant parts of our society. How can we learn to win and lose gracefully?**

Continue the meeting by having kids read and discuss Proverbs 27:1-4 and Matthew 5:3-10.

• Playing Favorites •

PURPOSE: *to discover what the Bible says about loving God and one another*

SCRIPTURE: *Matthew 22:37-40*

SUPPLIES: *a Bible, three colors of paper, safety pins, and volleyball equipment*

Give each teenager a safety pin and a sheet of paper—use all three colors equally. Have teenagers help each other pin the paper to their backs. Then say: **Form a huddle in your like-colored groups, and secretly choose one other color group to be your ally and one to be your enemy.**

When groups have chosen their allies and enemies, have kids form two teams to play volleyball. During the game, kids should be friendly to their allies and less friendly to their enemies. However, allow no verbal or physical abuse. After playing for a while, call time and have kids sit in like-color groups. Ask:

- **What was it like to support one color group and not the other?**
- **How do you feel toward the people who chose your color group as their enemy?**
- **What surprised you about the way people acted in this game?**
- **How is the way people treated each other like the way people act toward each other in real life?**

Have a volunteer read aloud Matthew 22:37-40. Continue with a discussion about what this passage teaches about relating to others and to God.

■ ■

▪ Centipede ▪

PURPOSE: *to learn how to be patient with one another*

SCRIPTURE: *1 Thessalonians 5:14*

SUPPLIES: *a Bible; masking tape; and plastic grocery bags, large rubber bands, rope, or strips of cloth*

Before class, use masking tape to mark a starting line and a finish line in a large, open space. Have group members stand side by side. Using the supplies you've gathered, have kids connect their legs with the people on both sides of them. Every person's legs should be connected to other people's legs—except for one person on each end, who will have only one leg connected to someone else's.

Say: **You're a many-legged centipede! Your goal is to walk to the finish line without your hands or knees touching the floor. If any hands or knees touch the floor, the centipede must return to the starting line and begin again.**

After the centipede reaches its goal (or after three minutes), have kids sit down. Ask:

● **How well did you work together to accomplish your goal?**

● **What were the secrets to your success in finally reaching your goal?**

Read aloud 1 Thessalonians 5:14. Then ask:

● **How did you see people warn those who didn't work in this game? encourage those who were afraid? help the weak?**

● **How was your patience tried in this game?**

● **Why does God encourage us to be patient with everyone?**

● **How can we apply this verse to the way we treat each other in our group?**

Pray together, asking God for help in being patient with each other, and when necessary, in warning, encouraging, or helping each other.

▪ Trust Me! ▪

PURPOSE: *to learn to trust God to guide them*

SCRIPTURE: *Psalms 40:4; 56:10-11; and Proverbs 3:5-6; 16:20*

SUPPLIES: *Bibles, blindfolds, sponges, and water*

Gather everyone in an open area, preferably on a grassy area outside. Have kids form pairs, blindfold one person in each pair, and give him or her a wet sponge. Explain that the blindfolded partners are the "players" and the other partners are the "coaches." Tell kids that on "go" the players will throw sponges at others by following their coaches' verbal commands such as "Right! Left! Duck! Run! Throw the sponge!" The coaches can only direct their players verbally—not by touch. If either partner gets hit by a sponge, both partners are out. After all the sponges are thrown, coaches can verbally guide their players to the sponges on the ground to continue the action. When only one pair is left, have partners switch roles and play again.

Have kids clean up the area and then gather for a brief discussion. Ask:

● **How did you feel as you were blindfolded and had to trust your friend to lead you?**

● **How do these feelings compare to your feelings as you trust God to guide you—even though you can't see God?**

● **What was it like to guide a blindfolded partner?**

● **How do you think these feelings are like or unlike God's feelings as he guides us?**

Pick four volunteers to read aloud these Scriptures: Psalm 40:4; Psalm 56:10-11; Proverbs 3:5-6; and Proverbs 16:20. Ask:

● **What do these Scriptures say to you about trusting God?**

● **Has there been a time when you trusted God? when you didn't trust God? Explain.**

Have a volunteer lead the group in a prayer asking for God's guidance and for a greater ability to trust God.

▪ Mission for God ▪

PURPOSE: *to follow assignments to learn what it means to follow God*

SCRIPTURE: *Jonah 1:1-3*

SUPPLIES: *Bibles*

Gather kids into groups of no more than four. Say: **Choose one person in your group to be the "captain." The rest of your group will be sending the captain out on strange assignments for the next few minutes.**

Have each group choose unusual things for its captain to do, such as stand on a chair and sing "Happy Birthday to You," make a cup of mud, and dust the room's furniture. Caution kids not to ask their captains to do anything inappropriate or unkind, such as kissing another group member or putting down someone else in the group.

After about three minutes, have each group choose a new captain and repeat the activity with new assignments. Continue until each person has been a captain.

Then have kids form a circle, read in unison Jonah 1:1-3, and discuss these questions:

● **How is the way you were sent on assignment like the way Jonah was sent? How is it different?**

● **How did it feel to accomplish your assigned tasks?**

● **Do you understand why Jonah ran away from his assignment? Explain.**

● **How can we follow God when we're given unusual or tough assignments?**

Continue asking kids for input and insight as they study Jonah's relationship with a loving and patient God.

▪ Psalm Scenes ▪

PURPOSE: *to appreciate the dramatic richness of the psalms*

SCRIPTURE: *Selected psalms*

SUPPLIES: *Bibles*

Form acting troupes of no more than five kids. Assign each troupe a psalm that portrays a dramatic scenario. For example, Psalm 8 portrays wonder; Psalm 23, comfort; Psalm 38, sickness;

Psalm 42, sadness; Psalm 66, thankfulness; Psalm 69, fear; Psalm 100, praise; and Psalm 109, anger.

Give troupes five minutes to read their psalms and create dramatic presentations of them. If time is short, each troupe can choose the part of its psalm that is the most dramatic and representative of the psalm's theme. For example, for Psalm 8, kids could portray the sheep, cattle, wild animals, birds, and fish.

Instruct each troupe to act out its psalm while a narrator reads the psalm aloud. After each troupe presents its drama, have the "audience" applaud in appreciation.

▪ Neighborly Chairs ▪

PURPOSE: *to play an action game while learning about love*

SCRIPTURE: *Luke 10:25-37; 1 Corinthians 13; and 1 John 4:7-21*

SUPPLIES: *none*

Form a circle of chairs that faces inward. Use one fewer chair than there are people. Instruct group members to sit down. The person without a chair must stand in the center of the circle.

Have the person in the middle ask someone, "Do you love your neighbor?" If the person answers "no," then that person and the people on either side of him or her must try to switch chairs and the person in the middle of the circle must try to get an empty chair. No one may return to his or her original chair. One person will always be left standing in the center of the circle.

If the person answers "yes," then that person must add, "and everyone who's wearing red" (or some other description). All people who fit the description must find a new seat.

After the game, have kids read Luke 10:25-37; 1 Corinthians 13; and 1 John 4:7-21 to provide biblical background for a discussion about love.

Devotional Openings

"And pray in the Spirit on all occasions with all kinds
of prayers and requests. With this in mind, be alert
and always keep on praying for all the saints."
EPHESIANS 6:18

Pray often with your group to help teenagers establish a deeper prayer life and grow spiritually. Start your meetings with devotional openers to get kids thinking about God and their spiritual lives. It's always appropriate to begin with prayer, regardless of what you have planned for the rest of the meeting.

■ ■

▪ Paper Hopes ▪

PURPOSE: *to share with God their hopes for the new school year*

SCRIPTURE: *Romans 5:3-5*

SUPPLIES: *paper, newsprint, masking tape, marker*

Give each student a sheet of paper. Ask kids to tear their paper into shapes that represent their hopes for the coming school year. For example, someone could hope for good grades and then tear an A shape, or someone could hope for new friends and then tear the shape of a person. When kids finish, have them explain their paper shapes.

On a sheet of newsprint, write, "Wall of Hopes"; then tape the newsprint to a wall. Have kids form a semicircle facing the wall. Set out a roll of tape. Tell kids to pray silently and offer God their hopes for the new school year. When kids have finished praying, ask them to tape their paper shapes to the Wall of Hopes. Then pray: **Dear God, work within us to help our hopes come true this year. Thanks for your loving presence each day of our lives. In Jesus' name, amen.**

▪ What's in a Name? ▪

PURPOSE: *to identify God's blessings in their lives*

SCRIPTURE: *Genesis 39:1-6a*

SUPPLIES: *a Bible, paper, and markers*

Give kids paper and markers, and ask them to print their names vertically down the left sides of their papers. Read aloud Genesis 39:1-6a. Say: **God blessed Joseph greatly, and God also has blessed each one of us.**

Have teenagers think of blessings that begin with the letters in their names and write the blessings next to the letters, as shown. You can help kids by suggesting they use "generic" blessings such as "home" or "family," specific names of relatives or friends such as "Uncle Bill" or "Chad," sports names, favorite foods, or names of their pets.

Give young people plenty of time to think of their many blessings. (It's OK if kids don't use some of the letters in their names.) Then have kids form pairs and discuss the blessings they listed.

■ ■

Encourage partners to pray for each other, thanking God for their blessings.

Encourage teenagers to keep their lists in a visible place at home so they can be reminded of God's constant love.

Music
A lan
R aquetball
I ce cream
A nimals

▪ I Am With You ▪

PURPOSE: *to empower kids to proclaim God's message*

SCRIPTURE: *Jeremiah 1:6-9*

SUPPLIES: *Bibles*

Ask kids to think of things that frighten them about Christian living or things they feel they can't do because they're too young or inexperienced, such as teaching Sunday school, telling others about Jesus, or reading aloud Scripture in worship services. Share an experience of your own to get things rolling.

When teenagers have had a few minutes to consider this, have them open their Bibles to Jeremiah 1:6-9. Read aloud the passage as kids follow along. Then have kids form pairs to discuss the following questions:

● **How did Jeremiah respond to his call as a prophet of God?**

● **Has God ever asked you to do something that made you feel the way Jeremiah did? If so, what did you do?**

Say: **Let's be honest with God about our fears and ask him to help us.** Pray: **God, sometimes the things you ask us to do are difficult for us. We don't feel worthy to bring your message of love and grace to others. It's overwhelming to be your messengers.**

Sometimes people don't want to listen. Sometimes we can't find the right words or actions. Give us strength to do your will and tell others of your love.

Ask volunteers to add their own prayers about fears or trials that they're experiencing. Then end the prayer by having the group read in unison God's words to Jeremiah in verses 7 and 8: "Do not say, 'I am only a child.' You must go to everyone I send you to and say whatever I command you. Do not be afraid of them, for I am with you and will rescue you."

• A Matter of Trust •

PURPOSE: *to learn about trusting God*

SCRIPTURE: *Genesis 22:1-14*

SUPPLIES: *Photocopies of the creative reading "The Lord Will Provide" (pp. 35-36)*

For the creative reading from Genesis 22:1-14, choose readers for the following roles: God, Abraham, Narrator, Isaac, and Angel of the Lord. A number of kids can play the role of Chorus. Distribute copies of "The Lord Will Provide" to the readers. Give everyone a few minutes to look over the creative reading, and then begin.

• "No" Answered Prayers •

PURPOSE: *to understand that God isn't rejecting them when he says no*

SCRIPTURE: *Deuteronomy 3:23-29*

SUPPLIES: *a Bible*

Have kids line up single file. Say: **I'm going to read some prayer requests. After each one, take one step to the left if you think God would give the person praying what he or she asked for. Take one step to the right if you think God would say no to the request.**

Read the following sample prayer requests, pausing after each one for kids to step left or right. Allow volunteers to explain why they stepped the direction they did. Read aloud:

● **Please give me a red convertible.**
● **Please comfort my grandmother while she's sick.**

The Lord Will Provide

God: "Abraham!"

Abraham: "Here I am."

God: "Take your son, your only son, Isaac, whom you love, and go to the region of Moriah. Sacrifice him there as a burnt offering on one of the mountains I will tell you about."

Chorus: "Offer right sacrifices and trust in the Lord" *(Psalm 4:5)*.

Narrator: "Early the next morning Abraham got up and saddled his donkey. He took with him two of his servants and his son Isaac. When he had cut enough wood for the burnt offering, he set out for the place God had told him about. On the third day Abraham looked up and saw the place in the distance. He said to his servants..."

Abraham: "Stay here with the donkey while I and the boy go over there. We will worship and then we will come back to you."

Chorus: "Those who know your name will trust in you, for you, Lord, have never forsaken those who seek you" *(Psalm 9:10)*.

Narrator: "Abraham took the wood for the burnt offering and placed it on his son Isaac, and he himself carried the fire and the knife. As the two of them went on together, Isaac spoke up and said to his father Abraham..."

Isaac: "Father?"

Abraham: "Yes, my son?"

Isaac: "The fire and the wood are here...but where is the lamb for the burnt offering?"

Abraham: "God himself will provide the lamb for the burnt offering, my son."

Narrator: "And the two of them went on together."

Chorus: "The Lord is my strength and my shield; my heart trusts in him, and I am helped" *(Psalm 28:7a)*.

Narrator: "When they reached the place God had told him about, Abraham built an altar there and arranged the wood on it."

Chorus: "Trust in the Lord with all your heart and lean not on your own understanding" *(Proverbs 3:5)*.

Narrator: "He bound his son Isaac and laid him on the altar, on top of the wood."

Chorus: "But I trust in you, O Lord" *(Psalm 31:14a)*.

Narrator: "Then he reached out his hand and took the knife to slay his son."

Chorus: "Surely God is my salvation; I will trust and not be afraid" *(Isaiah 12:2a)*.

Angel of the Lord: *(Loudly)* "Abraham! Abraham!"

Abraham: "Here I am."

Angel of the Lord: "Do not lay a hand on the boy...Do not do anything to him. Now I know that you fear God, because you have not withheld from me your son, your only son."

Narrator: "Abraham looked up and there in a thicket he saw a ram caught by its horns. He went over and took the ram and sacrificed it as a burnt offering instead of his son. So Abraham called that place The Lord Will Provide."

All: "To you, O Lord, I lift up my soul; in you I trust, O my God" *(Psalm 25:1-2a)*.

● Please let my little brother get laryngitis for the next five years.

● Please help my friend become a Christian.

● Please help me pass my test tomorrow, although I didn't study enough.

● Please help me ace my test tomorrow, since I studied so much for it.

● Please forgive my sins and give me eternal life.

Gather kids together, and ask: **How do you feel when God says no to your prayers?** Following a brief discussion, have someone read aloud Deuteronomy 3:23-29. Ask:

● **How do you think Moses felt when God told him no?**

● **How can we cope with our disappointment when God doesn't give us what we want?**

As a group, pray for each member one at a time, saying in unison, "God, please help (name) continue to trust you even when the answer's no."

▪ Power Trip ▪

PURPOSE: *to experience the power of prayer through a creative prayer service*

SCRIPTURE: *2 Kings 20:1-6*

SUPPLIES: *a Bible; a table; two candles; matches; index cards; pencils; a basket; and instrumental, meditative music*

Before teenagers arrive, set up a table. On the table, put two candles, a Bible opened to 2 Kings 20:1-6, and a basket. Turn on the meditative music, light the candles, and dim the lights. If possible, meet in a quiet place such as a prayer chapel.

As teenagers enter the room, ask them to remove their shoes and sit in chairs facing the table. After everyone is seated, explain that this is a creative prayer service. Give each person an index card and a pencil. Ask kids each to write a prayer request (they don't have to sign their names) and place the card face down in the basket. As each card is placed in the basket, have kids say together, "Hear our prayer, O Lord." After all the cards are in the basket, ask each person to silently come up to the table, turn over a card, and offer a prayer for what's on the card.

Have everyone pray silently for a few minutes. Then turn on the lights, and ask:

● **How did you feel when you entered the room?**
● **How did you feel during the service?**
● **What was it like to pray for someone else?**

Say: **When we pray, we develop a closer relationship with God. And there's power in prayer. Listen to this example from 2 Kings 20:1-6.**

▪ Prayer Bulletins ▪

PURPOSE: *to pray and be encouraged to keep track of answered prayers*

SCRIPTURE: *Matthew 5:44; Matthew 21:22; and Hebrews 4:16*

SUPPLIES: *a Bible, a bulletin board, newsprint, index cards, pencils, pushpins, markers, and tape*

Before kids arrive, cover a bulletin board with newsprint, and title it "Prayer Bulletins." On individual index cards, write the Scripture texts for Matthew 5:44; Matthew 21:22; and Hebrews 4:16. Pin these onto the board. You can have kids write additional texts as the weeks progress.

Give kids index cards and pencils, and ask them to write their prayer requests. They can rate their own requests as either "minor"—such as "I need to ace my chemistry test this week"—or "major"—such as "My aunt needs to be healed of cancer." Be sure each person uses one card for each request. After the cards are filled out, have kids pin them to the bulletin board.

At the start of each weekly meeting, have group members gather around the board and pray for the requests. Encourage kids to pray boldly but not presumptuously; that is, not assuming God will do something he hasn't promised to do.

As prayers are answered, use a red marker to write "YES" across each request that God answered yes. Tape the cards to the wall around the bulletin board. Also tape the requests around the board that God answered no to.

Encourage kids to update the Prayer Bulletins weekly by adding new requests to the board and placing old requests on the wall. After you have a sizable collection of cards, discuss this prayer activity. Ask:

■■■■■■■■■■■■■■■■■■■■■■■■■■■■■■■■■■■■■■

● How do you feel about the number of "yes" cards on the wall? the number of "no" cards?

● Does seeing the answered prayer cards encourage you to keep asking God for both minor and major things? Why or why not?

● Why doesn't God say yes to all our requests?

● How should we respond when God says no? when he says yes?

■ God's Good Gifts ■

PURPOSE: *to thank God for their favorite things*

SCRIPTURE: *James 1:17*

SUPPLIES: *a Bible, paper, and pencils*

Give each person a sheet of paper and a pencil. Have kids write at the top of their papers, "A Few of My Favorite Things." Then give kids three minutes to list some of their favorite things. After three minutes, have kids gather in a circle with their lists in hand.

Have kids look at what they've written and then close their eyes. Say: **With your eyes closed, think about the things you've written. How are they like gifts to you? Who gave you these gifts? Now pick out one gift on your list to thank God for. We each can offer a sentence prayer, thanking God for that one special gift.**

Have a volunteer read aloud James 1:17. Then ask each person in the circle to offer a sentence prayer of thanksgiving. You can begin the prayer by saying, for example, "Thank you, God, for the gift of my house."

■ Prayerful Posture ■

PURPOSE: *to understand true reverence for God*

SCRIPTURE: *Matthew 17:14; Philippians 2:9-11; and 1 Peter 5:6-7*

SUPPLIES: *a Bible and three worship songs*

Ask kids to distance themselves from each other for a personal time of prayer and worship. Read aloud Matthew 17:14, and then say: **During this first song, bow your heads.** Play your first song selection.

Following the song, read aloud Philippians 2:9-11, and then say: **During this second song, kneel and bow your heads.** Play the second song.

Then read aloud 1 Peter 5:6-7, and say: **During this third song, kneel and then lie flat with your faces to the floor.**

Following the third song, ask students to rise and gather together for reflection. Ask:

● **How do you define "reverence"?**

● **Did the posture you took reflect respect for God? Why or why not?**

● **Can we see God more clearly when we're truly humbled?**

● **In what ways can we humble ourselves before God each day?**

Ask volunteers to close in a prayer thanking God for Jesus' example of humility, obedience, and service.

▪ Silent Study ▪

PURPOSE: *to learn how to listen to God*

SCRIPTURE: *1 Kings 19:1-18*

SUPPLIES: *Bibles, newsprint, tape, marker, paper, pencils, and construction paper in colors as listed below*

Before class, write the following color chart on a sheet of newsprint, and tape the newsprint to a wall:

Color Chart

Green = Yes
Red = No
Blue = Read.
Yellow = Stand.
Brown = Sit.
Black = Pray silently.
Purple = Hug.
Light Blue = Write down your questions, if you have any.
White = Meditate on scriptural passage.
Pink = Take notes.

When everyone has arrived, distribute slips of green and red paper, a sheet of white paper, a pencil, and a Bible to each person.

■■■

Explain to kids that they must not speak during the activity. Tell them you'll hold up different colors of paper to communicate, as indicated by the color chart. Ask kids to read what you write on the newsprint and take notes on their papers. Tell kids that at the end of the activity, they will communicate with the red and green paper slips.

Following the directions below, hold up the appropriate colors one at a time. Allow a few minutes for each response.

1. Hold up brown paper.

2. Write, "1 Kings 19:1-3a" on newsprint, and then hold up blue paper.

3. Write, "How does Elijah feel?" Hold up white, then pink, then light blue paper.

4. Write, "1 Kings 19:3b-8." Hold up blue paper.

5. Write, "How does Elijah feel now?" Hold up white, then pink paper.

6. Write, "Why do you think the angel of the Lord visited Elijah?" Hold up white, then pink, then light blue paper.

7. Write, "1 Kings 19:9-13," and then hold up blue paper.

8. Write, "What did Elijah hear that brought him out of the cave?" Hold up white, then pink paper.

9. Write, "1 Kings 19:14-18," and then hold up blue paper.

10. Write, "What did the Lord say to Elijah?" Hold up white, then pink paper.

11. Write the following questions, one at a time, on newsprint. Have kids respond to each question by holding up the red or green paper. Write:

● Have you ever felt all alone?

● Have you ever been afraid?

● Have you ever looked for the Lord and not been able to find him?

● Have you ever heard the "gentle whisper" of the Lord speaking to you?

12. Hold up black paper. Bow your head for a silent prayer.

13. Hold up yellow paper, then purple paper. Have a quiet group hug.

In your meeting that follows, discuss any questions kids might have regarding Elijah's encounter with God or how they can listen to God.

Discussion-Starter Openings

"These commandments that I give you today are to
be upon your hearts. Impress them on your
children. Talk about them when you sit at home and
when you walk along the road, when you lie down
and when you get up."
DEUTERONOMY 6:6-7

*H*elp your teenagers learn to analyze facts, form opinions about issues, ask questions, and listen while others speak. Teach them God's
commands and how to look for answers to their questions in Scripture.
Use these thought-provoking openers to begin meetings on issues you
want your kids to discuss.

■ ■

▪ Lead On! ▪

PURPOSE: *to be nurtured as leaders*

SCRIPTURE: *1 Timothy 4:11-16 and 2 Timothy 2:22-26*

SUPPLIES: *Bibles, pencils, and paper*

Have kids form groups of three, and give each group a pencil, paper, and a Bible. Say: **All I can tell you is that we're supposed to study 1 Timothy 4:11-16 and 2 Timothy 2:22-26. Based on these passages, plan a meeting with at least three activities that we can all enjoy and learn from.**

Allow several minutes for groups to tackle the assignment. Some will go at it enthusiastically, while others may feel overwhelmed by the task. After several minutes, ask:

● **How does it feel to suddenly be in charge? Explain.**
● **What surprised you about having to plan a meeting?**
● **How could I have helped you do a better job?**
● **What are the risks of being a leader?**
● **How do you feel about teenagers being leaders?**

Say: **Each of you is a leader right now in one way or another.** Continue with a discussion about what it means to be a leader, using various groups' activity ideas.

▪ House of God ▪

PURPOSE: *to build an altar and create a "house of God"*

SCRIPTURE: *Genesis 28:10-22*

SUPPLIES: *Bibles, rocks, and markers*

Have each person bring a fist-sized rock to the meeting, or gather rocks yourself and have a few extra on hand. Tell kids to write their names on their rocks with markers.

Choose volunteers to read aloud Genesis 28:10-22, about Jacob's encounter with God at Bethel.

Have kids use their rocks to build an altar in a corner of the meeting room. Encourage kids to turn the room into a "Bethel," or "house of God," where they can leave their worries at the door and share their hearts openly. Have kids set up rules of behavior such as "No put-downs" or "Pray faithfully for others' concerns."

Keep the altar in the corner of the room as a reminder of the Bethel covenant.

▪ Listen Up! ▪

PURPOSE: *to learn that building a relationship with God involves learning to listen*

SCRIPTURE: *Psalm 46:10*

SUPPLIES: *a Bible*

Say: **Today we're going to learn about each other. You can tell your group about where you were born, members in your family, your favorite school subjects, your favorite sports, and so on.**

Have kids form trios and sit in circles. On "go," have kids begin telling about themselves simultaneously. Encourage kids each to talk louder than their partners so they alone can be heard.

After a minute, gather everyone together. Ask:

● **What did you learn about the people in your group?**

● **How did you feel trying to make everyone else hear your story?**

● **Did you try listening to their stories while you were talking? Why or why not?**

● **How do you think God feels if we "shout" requests at him but never take time to listen to him by meditating on his Word?**

● **Why might it be important just to sit quietly at times and listen for God to speak to us?**

Read aloud Psalm 46:10. Continue the meeting with a time of quiet reflection and then discussion. Ask kids for their insights and experiences on knowing God and being "still" before him.

▪ Making a Difference ▪

PURPOSE: *to discuss the impact they make in people's lives*

SCRIPTURE: *Acts 1:8*

SUPPLIES: *a Bible, a detailed map of your community, tape, a bulletin board, pushpins, index cards, and pencils*

Before class, tape a map of your community to a bulletin board.

Gather kids around the map, and ask them to think about their close relationships with people in their community, including relationships with family members and friends.

Read aloud Acts 1:8. Then say: **God has placed you in this community for a reason. God has placed people in your life to love** and help grow closer to God. Let's take a look at all the people we know who we can reach out to.

Have kids stick pushpins in the map to indicate where the people they can reach out to live.

Say: **Look at all the people we know!** Ask:

● **Have you ever thought of these people in terms of their need for God's love? Why or why not?**

● **What obstacles keep you from telling them about God's love?**

● **What obstacles keep you from doing something that will show them God's love?**

● **What can you do to impact one of these people for God this week?**

Tell each person to write the names of the people he or she thought of on an index card. Then have kids take their cards home as reminders of the people they are close to. Encourage kids to focus on making an impact for God in these people's lives over the next few months.

▪ No Place Like Home ▪

PURPOSE: *to value home and memories*

SCRIPTURE: *Ezra 1:1-7*

SUPPLIES: *Bibles and objects teenagers bring from home*

Before the meeting, ask each person to bring a favorite possession from home.

■■■

Have teenagers form groups of three or four. In their groups, have teenagers show their possessions and explain their personal value.

Allow time for small-group discussion of the following questions, and then have volunteers share their insights with the whole class. Ask:

● **What criteria did you use in selecting your object?**

● **What other objects might you have brought if you were allowed two or three items? Explain.**

● **How do the items you own contribute to making your house a "home"?**

● **Other than material goods, what makes your home special and valuable to you?**

Say: **For seventy years the Jews had been away from their homeland as captives in a foreign land. The Bible tells about the Jews' first opportunity to return home and be a nation again.** Have volunteers take turns reading Ezra 1:1-7. Ask:

● **What things would you miss about home if you had to be away for several decades?**

● **Would the object you chose to bring today still be as important? Explain.**

● **What would be the first thing you'd do when you finally returned home?**

● **According to these verses, what were some of the things the Jews did to prepare to return home?**

Encourage teenagers to discuss in their groups what items they'd select if they were to be gone for seventy years but were certain to return. Continue your study, focusing on the value of home and memories.

▪ Awesome Sight ▪

PURPOSE: *to think about and discuss Jesus' ascension and coming return*

SCRIPTURE: *Acts 1:7-14*

SUPPLIES: *Bibles and flashlights (optional)*

Take teenagers to an open area where they can sit comfortably and look up into the sky. If you meet at night, find an area away from the city lights so kids can see the stars. Have kids look into the sky for a few minutes. Ask them not to talk. Then ask:

- What do you think about when you look at the sky?
- What makes the sky mysterious?
- What mystery about our world do you wish you understood?

Give teenagers several more minutes to think and look at the sky; then read aloud Acts 1:7-11. Ask:

- What do you think the disciples were feeling as they watched Jesus being taken up into the sky? Explain.
- What promise is given in verse 11?
- How is the way you feel about the mysteries of our world like the way you feel about Jesus' return?

Have a volunteer read aloud Acts 1:12-14. Ask:

- What do you think these people prayed about when they were together?
- How does knowing that Jesus could return any moment affect how you live your life?

As they look into the sky, let kids take turns describing what it might be like if Jesus were to return at that very moment.

▪ Go for the Goal ▪

PURPOSE: *to grow closer to God*

SCRIPTURE: *James 4:7-8a*

SUPPLIES: *a Bible*

Have kids form a large circle by holding hands, moving back three or four steps, then dropping hands. Place a Bible in the center of the circle. Say: **As I read each of the following statements, I'll tell you whether you can move one step closer to the center or whether you must take one step back.**

Use the following statements or your own:

- Move one step closer if you've ever prayed for a friend.
- Move one step closer if you've ever prayed for a parent.
- Move one step back if you've ever broken one of the Ten Commandments.
- Move one step closer if you've ever told someone about God's love.
- Move one step back if you've ever made fun of a classmate at school.
- Move one step closer if you've ever fed or helped a stranger.

■ ■

● Move one step closer if you've ever believed in someone when nobody else would.

● Move one step back if you've ever pretended not to see someone in need.

● Move one step closer if you've ever been honest when it would have been easier to tell a lie.

Continue with instructions until someone reaches the Bible in the middle of the circle.

Have kids form pairs and discuss the following questions:

● How did you feel as you moved closer to the center of the circle?

● What did you notice about the group as the activity went on?

Have a volunteer pick up the Bible from the center of the circle and read James 4:7-8a. Ask:

● How do your actions affect your relationship with God?

● What do you think it means to submit to God?

Have teenagers form a close circle with their arms over one another's shoulders. Encourage kids to ask God to help them grow closer to him by honoring him in the things they do and say.

■ Whatever the Cost ■

PURPOSE: *to learn about giving up what they want to keep*

SCRIPTURE: *Matthew 16:24-26; Luke 18:22-25; and John 13:12-17*

SUPPLIES: *Bibles, chocolate kisses, and candy bars*

Show kids the chocolate kisses, but don't let them see the candy bars yet. Give each person a chocolate kiss. Then ask: **Who would like to give away the chocolate kiss I've just given you?**

Tell kids who volunteer to give up their candy to give the candy to others in the group. After they have done so, bring out the candy bars, and give them to the kids who gave up their kisses. If nobody gives a chocolate kiss away, bring out the candy bars and show kids what they missed.

Have kids form groups of four and read aloud Matthew 16:24-26 in their groups. Then ask group members to discuss these questions:

● How did it feel to give up your chocolate kiss? to not give it up?

■ ■

● Jesus says people must give up things to follow him. What kinds of things is Jesus talking about?

● What is Jesus asking us to do in this passage?

Gather kids together for further discussion and study of Luke 18:22-25 and John 13:12-17.

▪ No Glory ▪

PURPOSE: *to show through a skit how hard it can be to serve*

SCRIPTURE: *Luke 6:31-36 and John 13:1-17*

SUPPLIES: *a Bible, photocopies of the "Your Serve" handout (p. 50), and props for the skit as listed on the handout*

Following the skit, ask:

● **Do you agree with Gloria's statement that there's no glory in serving? Why or why not?**

● **How did the girls' actions demonstrate servanthood?**

● **What does this skit say about having a servant's heart?**

Use Luke 6:31-36 and John 13:1-17 as a springboard for a discussion on servanthood.

▪ Mind Readers ▪

PURPOSE: *to relate a guessing game to having the "mind of Christ"*

SCRIPTURE: *Romans 8:5-11 and 1 Corinthians 2:11-16*

SUPPLIES: *a Bible, paper, and pencils*

Have kids form two equal groups. Ask groups to line up along opposite walls in your meeting room, facing each other. Say: **Walk straight toward each other until you're standing across from one other person. The person you're now facing is your partner for this activity.**

Ask pairs to sit back to back. Tell partners to decide who'll be the "mind reader" and who'll be the "client." Hand each client a sheet of paper and a pencil.

Say: **Clients, you have one minute to think of a thought—any thought—and write it on your sheet of paper. When you're finished writing, fold the paper.**

(continued on p. 51)

Your Serve

Scene: Tanya and Gloria are cleaning up after helping their youth group paint the house of an elderly church member.

Props: You'll need a chair, a bucket of water, and towels. Also, both characters must wear shoes and socks for this skit.

Characters:

Tanya

Gloria

Script

(Tanya and Gloria enter, looking exhausted.)

Tanya: I'm really beat...

Gloria: Yeah, that hot sun really takes a lot out of you.

Tanya: *(Plopping down into a chair)* This servant stuff is really tough.

Gloria: You're telling me. *(She removes Tanya's shoes.)* It's all work and no play.

Tanya: Too much dirt and sweat, if you ask me.

Gloria: *(Helping Tanya remove her socks)* I thought it would make me feel good to help out.

Tanya: Me, too. I mean, I'm glad we're helping, but I just feel so tired and dirty.

Gloria: *(Gets a towel and begins to clean Tanya's feet using the water from the bucket.)* Yeah. I feel grubbier now than I felt after the youth group camping trip.

Tanya: *(Pointing to her feet)* And look at these feet! There's enough dirt here to plant a garden...

(Pause.)

Gloria: Do you think Mrs. Jordan appreciated our work today?

Tanya: Who knows? She doesn't think all that clearly these days, y'know. And she doesn't hear too well, either.

(Gloria finishes drying Tanya's feet, and then the two switch positions. Tanya removes Gloria's shoes and socks and then begins to clean her feet.)

Gloria: I'm not sure I want to come back tomorrow.

Tanya: I was thinking the same thing. I'm not cut out for this servant stuff. I really thought I'd feel good helping someone out. But it's not much fun if no one notices all the work we're doing...

Gloria: There's just no glory in serving.

(Characters freeze.)

■■■■■■■■■■■■■■■■■■■■■■■■■■■■■■■■■■■

After one minute, say: **Clients and mind readers, turn and face each other. Clients, give your mind readers your folded papers. Mind readers, put the papers to your foreheads, concentrate, and then tell your clients what they wrote. When you've guessed, open the papers to see if you were right.**

After all the mind readers have guessed, ask if anyone correctly guessed what was on his or her client's paper. Applaud those who happen to guess correctly. If you have time, have partners switch roles and repeat this activity.

Have kids gather together, and then ask:

● **Is it possible to read someone's mind? Why or why not?**

● **Mind readers, how did you feel as you tried to figure out what was on the papers?**

● **Clients, how did you feel when your mind readers tried to guess what you had written?**

Choose a volunteer to read aloud 1 Corinthians 2:11-16. Then ask:

● **How is the message of this passage like our mind reading experiment? different?**

● **What do you think it means to have the "mind of Christ"?**

Continue the discussion with kids, using related passages such as Romans 8:5-11, about how the Holy Spirit helps in our lives.

▪ We Doubt It! ▪

PURPOSE: *to learn about trusting Jesus*

SCRIPTURE: *John 20:24-31*

SUPPLIES: *a Bible*

Have kids form two teams. Say: **We're going to play a game called We Doubt It! Each of you will have a chance to tell something about yourself that's either true or false. For example, you could say, "My favorite food is my mom's fried chicken" or "I went to the school swimming meet on Friday night."**

The other team will try to guess if you're telling the truth. If they think you're lying, they'll say, "We doubt it." If they think you're telling the truth, they'll say, "We believe you." If you fool them, your team gets a point. If the other team guesses correctly, it gets a point.

■ ■

Alternate teams until each person has had a chance to tell something. Tally the score, and announce the winner. Ask:

● **What was it like to try to guess if someone was telling the truth?**

● **How is that like trying to decide whether to believe someone in real life?**

Ask a volunteer to read the story about Thomas in John 20:24-31. Then ask:

● **How is this game like trying to decide whether to believe what Jesus says? How is it different?**

Say: **Sometimes we aren't sure if we can believe people or not because we can't always be sure of their honesty or sincerity. But we know we can always trust what Jesus says.**

■ Headline News ■

PURPOSE: *to identify sins and talk about sin and forgiveness*

SCRIPTURE: *1 John 1:8-10*

SUPPLIES: *a Bible, newspapers, and markers*

Have kids form several small groups. Give each group a newspaper section and a marker. Ask groups to thumb through their sections and tear out articles about sins such as murder, theft, and lying. Have groups write the name of the sin across the front of each article. Then instruct each group to rank the sins it finds by arranging the articles on the floor, starting with the worst sin mentioned.

When everyone has finished, have a volunteer from each group tell about its sin rankings. Then ask:

● **How did your group decide which sins were worse than others?**

● **How does God view each sin?**

● **Does God rank sin? Explain.**

● **Would you refuse to forgive anyone you read about? Explain.**

Ask a volunteer to read aloud 1 John 1:8-10. Then say: **God thinks sin is sin—no matter what. But if anyone asks for forgiveness, he or she will receive it because God loves us. Today we're going to talk more about sin and forgiveness.**

· Our Eternal Home ·

PURPOSE: *to be assured of an eternal home with Jesus*

SCRIPTURE: *Matthew 8:18-20 and John 14:1-3*

SUPPLIES: *a Bible, paper, markers, and tape*

Before class, post signs on the doors of all the classrooms in the church. Each sign should say something like "No kids allowed," "Teenagers prohibited," or "Big kids, scram!" On one door, post a sign that says, "Can't you see there's no place for you here? Why don't you just leave!"

Meet group members in the parking lot.

Say: **There's a sign on the door of our room, so let's look for a different room for our meeting.**

Lead kids from door to door. When you come to the last door, say: **Well, maybe we should meet outside!**

Find a place to sit, and then have a volunteer read aloud Matthew 8:18-20. Ask:

● **How did you feel as we went from door to door?**

● **Jesus said he didn't have a place to call home. What do you think that felt like?**

● **Why do you think Jesus responded to the religious leader the way he did?**

Have a volunteer read aloud John 14:1-3. Ask kids to share what they learned from the passage about their eternal home.

■ ■

As you lead kids back to your room, have them help you remove the signs you posted.

Then say: **This is our room, and we're welcome here. It's "home" for our group. We can meet here and enjoy learning about the eternal home Jesus is preparing for us.**

Join together in thanksgiving for your heavenly home.

■ Fit for the Job ■

PURPOSE: *to discover what it means to be Christ's disciples*

SCRIPTURE: *Matthew 28:16-20*

SUPPLIES: *a Bible, paper, and pencils*

Have kids form groups of no more than four, and give each group a pencil and paper. Ask each group to list qualifications for a different line of work, such as a writer, police officer, or computer programmer. Tell kids to pretend they're responsible for hiring the best person for the job. Encourage them to be realistic about the qualifications and to be as specific as possible.

When kids have completed their lists, have a volunteer from each group read the group's list. Ask other group members to offer suggestions to make the qualifications as realistic as possible. Ask:

● **What determines if someone is qualified for a particular job?**

● **What happens when someone is hired who doesn't match the job requirements?**

Then have groups spend three minutes listing the qualifications to be a disciple of Jesus. Have a different person from each group read this list aloud.

Choose a volunteer to read aloud Matthew 28:16-20. Say: **The qualifications for being a disciple are few—you must be called by God and be willing to follow Jesus. But living out the "job" of a disciple isn't so simple. Today we're going to explore what it means to be a disciple.**

■ Test Your Faith ■

PURPOSE: *to learn that our "actions" don't make us Christians*

SCRIPTURE: *2 Corinthians 13:5 and Ephesians 2:8-10*

■■■

SUPPLIES: *a Bible, newsprint, a marker, tape, photocopies of "The Test of True Faith" handout (p. 56), and pencils*

Before class, write on newsprint the following chart. You will post the chart toward the end of the opening activity.

Number of "True" Answers

0 to 1 = Ouch!
2 to 4 = O ye of little faith
5 to 7 = Lukewarm
8 to 10 = The Pharisees are looking for a few new recruits!

Give each person a "Test of True Faith" handout and a pencil. Have kids complete the test by honestly answering the questions with "true" or "false." Assure kids that no one else will see their tests.

After kids have finished, have them score their tests by adding up the number of "true" answers. Then post the chart you made before the meeting. Point to it, and ask:

● **Does your score seem satisfactory? Explain.**

● **If you got a similar number of "right" answers on a test at school, what would your grade be?**

● **How do we "fail" this test of faith in everyday life?**

Say: **There's one more question on this test. On the line before "Bonus question," write "true" or "false" for this statement: I have committed my life to Jesus Christ and want to follow him in all I do.**

Read aloud 2 Corinthians 13:5, and then say: **If you answered "true" to the bonus question, according to 2 Corinthians 13:5, you passed the test of faith! The first ten questions, while important parts of the Christian life, do *not* make you a Christian. In fact, someone can practice *all* of these and not be a true Christian at all. The Pharisees tried to practice these things perfectly and yet were considered Christ's enemies.**

Choose a volunteer to read aloud Ephesians 2:8-10. Then ask:

● **How does your answer to the bonus question make you feel?**

● **What implications does this question have for the other ten questions?**

● **How can we act on our decision to follow Christ?**

Close in a prayer of thanksgiving for your students and their decisions to follow Jesus.

The Test of True Faith

Answer "true" or "false."

_____ 1. I study the Bible every day.

_____ 2. I attend church regularly.

_____ 3. I'm not afraid to pray aloud in front of others.

_____ 4. I listen carefully to sermons in church and try to apply them to my life.

_____ 5. I stand up against sin and ungodliness.

_____ 6. I understand basic theological truths.

_____ 7. I have a hunger for worship and prayer.

_____ 8. I'm involved in youth group activities and leadership.

_____ 9. I tell others about my faith.

_____ 10. I frequently sacrifice things for God, such as time and money.

_____ Score (total of "true" answers)

_____ Bonus question

▪ Who's the Best? ▪

PURPOSE: *to hold a bragging contest and learn about pride*

SCRIPTURE: *2 Chronicles 26:16-21 and Proverbs 16:18*

SUPPLIES: *a Bible*

Gather kids together, and say: **We're going to determine who's the best person here by having a bragging contest. Let's have each person complete the following sentence: "I'm the best because..." You may say something true, such as "I'm the best because I have the highest score in my math class." Or you may pretend and say something like, "I'm the best because the Chicago Bulls tried to recruit me for their team last week." Listen to what others say because we'll be voting for the best bragger.**

■■

Begin the bragging yourself, and then have kids take turns telling others why they're great. After everyone has had a chance to brag, have kids vote for the top four braggers. Then have these four go into the championship round. Give them one more chance to tell everyone why they're the best. After this round, have everyone vote once more to determine the group's best bragger.

Have the winner read 2 Chronicles 26:16-21 to the rest of the group. Ask:

● **Uzziah was a powerful king. What was his attitude toward God after he became great?**

● **When we think we're the best—whether it's true or not—what's our attitude toward God and others?**

● **What's it like to be around someone who's prideful?**

● **Do you ever have a problem with pride? Explain.**

Choose a volunteer to read aloud Proverbs 16:18. Ask:

● **How was this true for Uzziah?**

● **How is it true for us today?**

Have each person take a turn again, but this time in prayer. Have kids complete the sentence "God, you're the best because..." and "brag" to God about himself.

▪ Staying Strong ▪

PURPOSE: *to compare their temptation to Jesus' temptation*

SCRIPTURE: *Luke 4:1-13*

SUPPLIES: *a Bible and a variety of tempting snacks such as brownies, pizza, or a bowl of M&M's*

Before the meeting, place the treats on a table in the front of your meeting room. Have an adult volunteer ready to interrupt your meeting at the appropriate time.

As kids enter the room, explain that the snacks are for later. Begin leading the group in a crowdbreaker game. Just as the group starts the game, have your volunteer come to the room and call you out for a moment. Step away from the room for several minutes, closing the door behind you.

When you return, quietly note whether any snacks are missing. Have the group finish the game, and then call everyone together.

Have a volunteer read aloud Luke 4:1-13. Ask:

■ ■

● Were you tempted when I left the room?

● How was your temptation similar to what Jesus endured? How was it different?

If some kids did sneak food, give them the opportunity to share how they feel about doing this. Discuss how Jesus withstood temptation. Have kids share ways they avoid or stand up to temptations each day.

■ Jesus, Remember Me ■

PURPOSE: *to discuss forgiveness for criminals*

SCRIPTURE: *Matthew 6:14-15 and Luke 23:40-43*

SUPPLIES: *Bibles, "wanted" posters (available from law enforcement agencies), and pencils*

Have kids form groups of three or more. Give each group a "wanted" poster and a pencil. Ask groups to discuss the following questions and write their answers on the back of their posters:

● **What's an appropriate punishment for the person on this poster?**

● **Should forgiveness be an option? Why or why not?**

● **How could forgiveness be offered in this situation?**

● **Imagine that someone in our group was this person's victim. Now imagine that the judge gave you the right to choose the punishment. What would you choose?**

Say: **Often our first reaction is to punish people who hurt us. But that doesn't make the pain go away. Forgiveness can free us and others from bitterness and anger. Forgiveness is the bridge that leads from bitterness to freedom. Forgiveness means: (1) admitting you're hurt, (2) recognizing why you don't want to forgive, and (3) making the choice to forgive.**

Together, read Matthew 6:14-15 and Luke 23:40-43, and continue with a study on biblical forgiveness.

Getting-to-Know-You Openings

"Dear friends, since God so loved us,
we also ought to love one another."
1 JOHN 4:11

The better your teenagers know each other, the more they can help each other on their journeys of spiritual growth, faith-building, and discovery. Use these openings to help kids in your group get acquainted or get to know each other better. And encourage your teenagers to be loving and welcoming, just as Jesus is.

▪ Time Commitment ▪

PURPOSE: *to spend time with each other and commit to spending time with God*

SCRIPTURE: *Mark 6:45-46*

SUPPLIES: *Bibles, a watch or timer, paper, pencils*

Have kids form groups of no more than four. Allow each group member one minute to ask questions to learn as much as possible about the other kids in the group. Kids can ask questions about group members' families, favorite school subjects, favorite sports, and other personal likes and dislikes. Continue calling "time" after one minute until each person has had a turn. Then distribute paper and pencils to each person, and tell kids to write what they remember about the others in their groups. Give each person one more minute to confirm information or ask additional questions. Then ask:

● **How much did you learn about each other in the first minute?**

● **Did you learn anything new in the second minute? What?**

● **What might you learn about each other if you had five minutes a day to spend talking together?**

Ask kids to form pairs. Have partners read together Mark 6:45-46. Ask the group:

● **What does this passage say about spending time with God?**

● **What are some ways we can spend time with God?**

Have partners each choose one way they'll spend time with God daily. Then ask partners to check up on each other during the week for mutual encouragement.

▪ Loving Each Other ▪

PURPOSE: *to share what they love about others*

SCRIPTURE: *1 John 4:7-8*

SUPPLIES: *a Bible, a tennis ball, newsprint, and a marker*

Ask your group to sit in a circle. Explain that you're going to toss a tennis ball to someone across the circle; the receiver should then toss the ball to another person; that person should toss the ball to someone else; and so on.

Encourage kids to continue the same toss-and-catch pattern. Then ask kids each to name one thing they really "love"—such as basketball, skiing, french fries, or movies—as they toss the ball to the next person in the pattern.

To conclude the game, ask kids each to name one thing they really love about the person they're tossing the ball to (this will probably be much more difficult). Kids might name things such as a smile, friendliness, laugh, and sense of humor.

After the game, read aloud 1 John 4:7-8. Ask:

● **Why is it so important to love each other?**

● **How did you feel when someone told you something he or she loved about you?**

● **Why is it easier to talk about things we love than about what we love in others?**

● **What's one thing we can do in our group to show we love each other?**

Write kids' answers to the last question on newsprint. Have kids vote on the ideas and then put the best idea into action at a future meeting.

• Physical Mathematics •

PURPOSE: *to get acquainted during a crazy contortion game*

SCRIPTURE: *1 Corinthians 12:14-20*

SUPPLIES: *Bibles and prizes*

Have kids form teams of five for this crazy contortion crowd-breaker. Then ask kids each to say their names and something they like about math.

Say: **Now we're going to play Physical Mathematics—a game you're all going to like! First I'll ask a question; then you and your teammates will arrange yourselves on the floor to form the answer.**

Ask the following questions to help kids get to know each other better:

● **What's the total number of times your team has brushed its teeth today?**

● **What's the total number of slices of bread your team has eaten today?**

● **What's the total number of prayers your team has said today?**

Then ask volunteers to read aloud 1 Corinthians 12:14-20, and have kids discuss how they can work together as one team.

Grant an award to honor each team in categories such as "best contortionists," "quality teamwork," and "mathematical geniuses."

▪ Make-a-Friend Contest ▪

PURPOSE: *to explore building a friendship with Jesus*

SCRIPTURE: *John 15:13-15*

SUPPLIES: *a Bible, a birthday card, and a cupcake*

Give kids one minute to ask as many people as possible what their birthdays and favorite foods are—no writing allowed. Then see which person can remember correctly the most birthdays and favorite foods. Award a birthday card and cupcake to the winner.

Then say: **If making friends was as easy as asking for a person's birth date and favorite food, we'd always have plenty of friends. But making new friends involves more than just asking questions, especially when that friend is God.**

Ask a volunteer to read aloud John 15:13-15.

Say: **Just as we found out new things about each other today, we can learn more about building a friendship with Jesus and serving him.**

· Jesus Knows All ·

PURPOSE: *to see how much they know about their partners and realize that Jesus knows everything about them*

SCRIPTURE: *John 4:5-30*

SUPPLIES: *Bibles, paper, and, pencils*

Ask kids to choose partners and sit back to back. Give each person a pencil and a sheet of paper.

Say: **In this activity, we're going to see how well you know your partner. Some people may have the advantage of knowing their partners better than others, but do the best you can in answering the questions.**

Read aloud the following questions. Without allowing kids to confer with their partners, have them write their answers on their papers.

● **What is your partner's full name?**
● **On what street does your partner live?**
● **Does your partner have a job? If so, what does he or she do?**
● **What is your partner's favorite radio station?**
● **When was the last time your partner brushed his or her teeth?**
● **What's your partner's shoe size?**
● **What was the first name of your partner's first-grade teacher?**

Have kids talk over their answers with their partners and count how many questions they correctly answered.

Say: **It's impossible for any of us to know everything about another person. There are some things we don't even know about ourselves! Let's read about a woman who found someone who did know all about her.**

Ask for volunteers to read aloud John 4:5-30. Then have your group discuss what Jesus knew about the Samaritan woman and compare this to what Jesus knows about us. Also discuss how that might affect the way we live.

Say: **Jesus loved this woman in spite of the wrong things she'd done and in spite of the prejudice others held against her. He knew her, and he loved her. This is the same way he knows and loves each of us.**

• Affirmation Labels •

PURPOSE: *to help kids see the good in others and in themselves*

SCRIPTURE: *1 Peter 1:22-2:1*

SUPPLIES: *a Bible, self-adhesive name tags, and pens*

As teenagers enter the room, place a blank, self-adhesive name tag on each person's back. When everyone has arrived, hand out pens and encourage kids to write one positive, descriptive word on each group member's name tag. Tell kids that no word can be used twice on the same name tag.

When kids have written on each person's tag, have teenagers form a circle on the floor. Ask kids to remove their name tags and read what others have written about them. Choose a volunteer to read aloud 1 Peter 1:22-2:1. Then say: **We can train our hearts to see the good—not just the bad—in others. And with the help of the Holy Spirit, we can be true friends as Jesus wants us to be.**

Tell group members to take their name tags home as reminders of the good things others see in them.

• Mingle-Jingle •

PURPOSE: *to make friends*

SCRIPTURE: *Proverbs 18:24*

SUPPLIES: *a Bible, index cards, and a pen*

Before class, write the following jingles on separate index cards:
● "Hey! I'm glad you came. Hope you have a good time."
● "What's happening? You'll have to tell me all about it."
● "Have you heard the latest? If you've got a minute, I'll tell you."

After teenagers arrive, give three kids the "mingle-jingle" cards. Encourage these three kids to practice saying each jingle in a radio-announcer style. Say to the group: **We're going to spend time mingling before we start our meeting. Three people have mingle-jingles. When one of them says a mingle-jingle to you, you must repeat it to one other person, who will repeat it to someone else, and so on. For those of you who aren't saying a mingle-jingle, very quietly mutter, "Mingle, mingle, mingle" until someone says a mingle-jingle to you. Then repeat that mingle-jingle to someone else and continue muttering, "Mingle, mingle, mingle."**

■■

After three minutes of mingling, bring kids together, and say: **This silly activity shows that we can talk a lot but say very little. And that's no way to make friends. We're going to talk today about how to meet and make friends.** Read aloud Proverbs 18:24, and then ask:

● **How easy or difficult is it to meet new friends? Explain.**

● **How easy or difficult is it to know what to say to new friends? Explain.**

You might continue your meeting by exploring the friendships of David and Jonathan, Ruth and Naomi, and Paul and Timothy.

▪ Let's Give Them a Hand ▪

PURPOSE: *to learn about giving and receiving encouragement*

SCRIPTURE: *Isaiah 41:13*

SUPPLIES: *a Bible and blindfolds*

Before class, clear the room of any obstacles that might trip or injure blindfolded group members.

After everyone has arrived, have kids form pairs, and have partners choose to be the encourager or the seeker. Have the encouragers blindfold the seekers. After all blindfolds are in place, count to ten while the encouragers spin the seekers around.

When you've finished counting, say: **I want the encouragers to move quietly to the edges of the room and remain perfectly silent. Then I want the seekers to go in search of their partners. Walk carefully and slowly and keep talking so the other seekers know where you are. Once you find your partner, you can remove your blindfold.**

After kids have been searching for their partners for a few minutes, say to the encouragers: **Now I want you to call out to your partner and guide him or her to you using only your voice. When your partner gets close to you, grab his or her hand.**

Continue the activity until all the pairs are together. Have the group form a circle. Ask the seekers:

● **What was it like for you to try to find your partner without any help?**

● **How is that like trying to find encouragement when you feel down?**

Ask the encouragers:

● **What was it like to watch your partners try to find you without being able to help?**

● **How did you feel when you could call to them?**

● **How did you feel when you could finally grasp their hands?**

● **How is that like trying to encourage your friends when they're down?**

Choose a volunteer to read aloud Isaiah 41:13. Ask:

● **How do you think God tries to encourage you?**

● **How does receiving God's encouragement help you to encourage others?**

Ask volunteers to close in prayer, thanking God for his guidance and encouragement.

■ Lifelines ■

PURPOSE: *to create time lines to share important people and events in their lives*

SCRIPTURE: *Psalm 139*

SUPPLIES: *Bibles, butcher paper, tape, paint, markers, crayons, paper scraps, glue, scissors, and magazines*

Tape a continuous roll of butcher paper around the walls of your meeting room. If you have a large group, tape two levels of paper around the room. Set out the supplies, and ask everyone to choose a space on the butcher paper that is several feet wide.

Say: **Today we're each going to make a time line of our lives. You can paint, draw, or glue magazine pictures representing your life on the paper.** Tell kids to start with their births and create pictures of events, people, and places that were important while they grew up. When they're done, have kids tell their names and share their lifelines with the whole group.

Ask for volunteers to read aloud Psalm 139. Discuss God's care for us throughout our lives.

■ Great Expectations ■

PURPOSE: *to get acquainted, leading into a discussion about parents' expectations*

SCRIPTURE: *Exodus 20:12*

SUPPLIES: *a Bible, photocopies of the "Expectations Autographs" handout (p. 68), and pens*

Give each person a photocopy of the "Expectations Autographs" handout. Allow ten minutes for kids to get others to sign the blanks that apply to them. Afterward, have a volunteer read aloud Exodus 20:12. Then have teenagers discuss what they think about parents' expectations.

· Family Portrait ·

PURPOSE: *to serve as a crowdbreaker for a parents' night*

SCRIPTURE: *none*

SUPPLIES: *a prize*

Use this crowdbreaker at a parents' night so people can learn who belongs to who.

Have kids form a circle and face clockwise (siblings should be together). Have parents form a larger circle around the kids and face counterclockwise (spouses should be together). If some kids' parents aren't at the meeting, designate youth sponsors as parents or pair parent-kid teams.

On "go," instruct kids to walk clockwise and parents to walk counterclockwise around them. When you call out, "Family portrait," kids and their parents must find each other as quickly as possible and stand together, cheek to cheek and grinning. The last family to do this is out.

Keep playing until only one family is left. Declare the winners, and award a prize such as an instant-print photo or a picture frame.

· Looking Ahead ·

PURPOSE: *to help kids discover that their future is in God's hands*

SCRIPTURE: *Colossians 1:9-14*

SUPPLIES: *Bibles, paper, tape, and pencils*

As kids arrive, tape a sheet of paper to each person's back and hand each person a pencil.

Say: **Today we're going to get acquainted by predicting each**

Expectations Autographs

My parent expects me to

- walk the dog. _____
- wait until I'm older to date. _____
- clean my room. _____
- go to church every Sunday. _____
- do my laundry. _____
- make my lunch. _____
- baby-sit my sibling(s). _____
- do the dishes. _____
- pay my phone bill. _____
- take the bus. _____
- get straight A's. _____
- work for spending money. _____
- watch my language. _____
- stay home on school nights. _____
- keep a curfew. _____

other's futures. Go around and jot on everyone's sheet of paper predictions about what that person's life will be like when he or she is forty-five. List information about occupations, hobbies, and family members. List only positive things. For example, you may write that someone is an astronaut who loves deep-sea diving and has ten children.

When kids are finished, have them look at what others predicted about their lives at the age of forty-five. Ask:

- **How accurate do you think these predictions will be?**

■ ■

● **Which predictions fit with your ideas about God's purposes for your life?**

● **Which predictions don't fit?**

Have volunteers read aloud Colossians 1:9-14, and then lead kids in a discussion about God's purpose for them.

▪ Letter Perfect ▪

PURPOSE: *to help group members learn each other's names*

SCRIPTURE: *none*

SUPPLIES: *none*

Place chairs in a horseshoe shape. After everyone is seated, start at one end of the horseshoe and give each person a different letter of the alphabet. If you have more than twenty-six kids, assign twenty-six kids a letter of the alphabet, and then assign the others a vowel—A, E, I, O, U, and Y. If you have a smaller group, assign two letters per person or assign letters that are frequently used, such as vowels and the consonants C, D, G, H, L, N, P, R, S, and T.

Select words ahead of time that will use each person's assigned letter at least once. Use kids' names and choose words that coincide with a topic such as care, God, holy, and so on.

After everyone has been assigned a letter, say: I'll call out a word or name. Those people assigned the letters in that word or name will run to the front of the group, stand in line—reading from left to right—and form their letters with their bodies.

Allow kids to be creative when making their "body letters." They'll have a great time!

▪ Shuffle the Deck ▪

PURPOSE: *to get acquainted*

SCRIPTURE: *none*

SUPPLIES: *a deck of cards*

Before class, pick out one playing card per person. Make sure you pick same-numbered cards in all suits. For example, if you have twelve kids in your group, choose the six through eight cards in all suits.

■■■

Mix the cards, and then give one to each person. Say: **To help us get acquainted, I'm going to read some instructions. Listen carefully so that you can follow the directions.** Say:

● **Find everyone with the same card number. Introduce yourselves, and then describe a favorite hobby you enjoyed when you were the same age as your card number.**

● **Find the person with the same card color and number, introduce yourselves, and find an object in the room that has your color or number on it.**

● **Find everyone with the same suit—hearts, clubs, spades, or diamonds. Introduce yourselves, then build a human sculpture that communicates this meeting's theme of** (name of theme).

Have groups explain their completed sculptures.

▪ Island Survival ▪

PURPOSE: *to see how well they know each other*

SCRIPTURE: *none*

SUPPLIES: *pencils and index cards or paper*

Give each person an index card and a pencil. Have each person write his or her name on the card and number the card from one to ten.

Say: **You've been assigned a top-secret mission on a deserted island. You'll be by yourself for a whole year with no opportunity to leave the island. For numbers one through five, list five things you'll want to have with you.**

Let kids know that their answers will be read aloud, and then give kids a few minutes to fill in their top five things. Ask:

● **For number six, if someone washed up on shore, who would you like it to be?**

● **For number seven, if a care package washed ashore, would you want it to be a pizza, a gallon of ice cream, or a dozen doughnuts?**

● **For number eight, if you heard strange sounds during the night, what would scare you the most: a large, wild, hungry boar; your little brother, who arrived on the island and is making those annoying noises; or a possible rescue boat leaving the island?**

● **For number nine, if your youth leader came to visit halfway** through your yearlong adventure, what would he or she say to you?

● For number ten, if you found out that Hollywood was going to make a movie about your adventure, who would play your part?

Collect all the index cards. Read each card, and have kids guess whose card you're reading.

▪ A Spy for a Spy ▪

PURPOSE: *to meet new group members*

SCRIPTURE: *none*

SUPPLIES: *a prize*

Before you begin, secretly choose three kids to be spies. Give them the code names "Pink Panther," "007," and "Maxwell Smart."

Explain to the group that its mission is to find the three spies. Say: **As you mingle, approach a person, shake hands, and ask his or her name. Then, while still holding hands, ask the person if he or she is either the Pink Panther, 007, or Maxwell Smart. You may ask only one code name at a time. A "no" response is one squeeze of the hand; a "yes" response is two squeezes of the hand.**

When you catch a spy, don't reveal the spy's identity; just continue introducing yourself to others. If you think you have discovered the true identities of all three spies, report to me.

Keep playing until most kids have identified at least two of the spies correctly.

▪ Cracker Jack Bob ▪

PURPOSE: *to get to know one another*

SCRIPTURE: *none*

SUPPLIES: *Cracker Jacks and a large bowl or bucket*

Ahead of time, purchase one box of Cracker Jacks for each group member. Empty the boxes of Cracker Jacks into a large bowl.

Ask kids to wash their hands before the activity. Tell them that instead of bobbing for apples in a tub of water, they're going to "bob" for prizes in a tub of Cracker Jacks using their hands.

As each person takes a turn, have the rest of the kids shout his or her name with encouraging cheers. Let everyone have a turn so all kids learn names and get prizes.

▪ Pet Talk ▪

PURPOSE: *to let their pets "do the talking" as they learn more about one another*

SCRIPTURE: *none*

SUPPLIES: *paper and pencils*

Tell kids they get to play a guessing game about their pets. Distribute paper and pencils, and ask kids each to write down the names of their pets. (If someone doesn't have a pet, tell them to choose a name for a pretend pet.)

Then have kids form teams of three or more. Call the teams, one by one, to stand in front of the others. Collect the kids' papers, and read aloud the names of three pets. Have kids guess which pet names belong to which team members. Repeat the process until all teams have finished.

Your group is sure to discover hilarious pet names and learn new secrets about one another.

▪ Junk Mixer ▪

PURPOSE: *to talk with each other*

SCRIPTURE: *none*

SUPPLIES: *small household items (see suggestions below), a pen, a sheet of paper, envelopes, pencils, and photocopies of the "junk" list*

Before the meeting, collect ordinary, small household items such as a button, eraser, rubber band, craft stick, thimble, pencil, and emery board. You'll need one item for each group member. Put each item in an envelope. List the items on a sheet of paper with a line beside each item. Make one photocopy of the "junk" list for each participant.

As kids arrive, hand them each an envelope, a photocopied list, and a pencil. Explain that each group member must somehow wear his or her item. Instruct kids to find out who's wearing each item and write that person's name on the list.

Youth-Issue Openings

"No temptation has seized you except what is common to man. And God is faithful; he will not let you be tempted beyond what you can bear. But when you are tempted, he will also provide a way out so that you can stand up under it."
1 CORINTHIANS 10:13

Teenagers face many temptations and often have to deal with problems related to dating, underage drinking, school, families, gangs, and even AIDS and abortion. They need to talk about these things, and they need someone who will listen and guide them. Use these openings to tackle some tough issues during your meetings.

▪ Making Impressions ▪

PURPOSE: *to open a discussion on peer pressure*

SCRIPTURE: *Proverbs 23:15-21*

SUPPLIES: *Bibles, thick crayons, and paper*

Give each person a sheet of paper and a crayon. Tell kids they have ten minutes to collect ten "impressions" of both the inside and the outside of the meeting area. Have kids place their sheets of paper over objects such as carpet, a heater grate, or a keyhole and rub their crayons on the paper. Tell kids to list each item they make an impression of on the back of their papers. When kids return, have them take turns guessing what objects the impressions are of. Then ask:

● **How could you determine the pattern that would appear on your paper?**

● **How could you avoid patterns that you didn't want on your paper?**

Ask kids to form pairs and read Proverbs 23:15-21.

Then say: **Sometimes we're like these sheets of paper, allowing others to make impressions on us. Our friends sometimes pressure us to look and act certain ways.** Have pairs discuss the following questions and then share insights with the whole class. Ask:

● **What are ways we can avoid negative peer pressure—the temptation to join our friends in disobeying God?**

● **Why are we sometimes attracted to what our friends are doing?**

● **How can we make positive impressions on our friends?**

Pray together that God will make his impression on all group members and that group members, in turn, will make God's impression on others.

▪ That's Not True! ▪

PURPOSE: *to feel the pain gossip can inflict*

SCRIPTURE: *Romans 1:28-32 and 1 Timothy 5:13*

SUPPLIES: *Bibles, index cards, a marker, and tape*

Before the meeting, write on five index cards five different gossip-starting phrases such as "Eats spaghetti in the bathtub," "Wears army boots to bed," or "Has a secret crush on Kermit the Frog."

■ ■

As kids come in, tape each card to the back of a different person. Don't let the kids know what the phrases on their backs say.

Encourage other group members to be "gossipmongers" and talk about the people "behind their backs." Have the gossipmongers begin their rumors with the phrases on the kids' backs and continue to feed the gossip by saying things like, "And that's not all. I heard she..." Be sure kids keep the "gossip" silly—not hurtful.

After five minutes, have everyone sit in a circle. Ask:

● How did those of you with cards on your backs feel as people gossiped about you?

● How did the rest of you feel as you gossiped?

● Have you ever been the object of gossip? Explain.

● How did you respond to the gossip?

Continue the discussion using Romans 1:28-32 and 1 Timothy 5:13 as a scriptural basis.

▪ Dark Days ▪

PURPOSE: *to discuss how to share hope with people who have AIDS*

SCRIPTURE: *Jonah 1:17–2:9*

SUPPLIES: *a Bible*

Dim the lights or take the group to a darkened room, and sit together in the darkness.

Say: **As yet, there's no cure for AIDS. If you get AIDS, you may live for several years or for only a few months. But eventually the virus weakens the body's immune system, and you die.** Ask:

● **What dark time have you experienced in your life?**

● **How would getting AIDS be like walking into a dark room?**

● **If you were in this dark room very long, how would it affect you?**

● **What are ways we can bring light into the life of someone who has AIDS?**

Read aloud Jonah 1:17–2:9. Ask:

● **How could someone with AIDS feel as if they'd been swallowed up as Jonah was?**

● **What did Jonah admit to God in his prayer?**

● **What are words of hope from Jonah's prayer that you could give to someone with AIDS?**

Turn up the lights, and close with a prayer similar to the following:

God, give us your grace to bring Christian compassion to AIDS sufferers. In Jesus' name, amen.

▪ What We're Looking For ▪

PURPOSE: *to think about how Jesus can meet gang members' needs*

SCRIPTURE: *John 10:10; 15:12-17; and Romans 12:9-10*

SUPPLIES: *string or tape and three bags filled with snacks*

Before the meeting, suspend three bags of snacks from the ceiling in different parts of your meeting room.

Have kids form three groups. Tell each group to get a bag of snacks, but don't give any further instructions.

When the groups have successfully taken down their snacks, ask a volunteer from each group to describe the group's method. Highlight any differences in groups' methods, and ask kids to suggest other ways they might have gone about getting the snacks—for example, by climbing on furniture, boosting each other up, or using a broom to knock the bag to the floor.

Say: **You all wanted the same thing, but you found different ways of getting it.** Ask:

● **Do you think gang members are looking for the same things in life that you are? Why or why not?**

Say: **Today we're going to look at some things most people want: love, hope, acceptance, and family. We're going to see how some people try to get those things through gangs, and how others find what they need through Jesus Christ.**

▪ The "In" Crowd ▪

PURPOSE: *to experience being included or excluded*

SCRIPTURE: *Mark 2:15-17*

SUPPLIES: *a Bible, scissors, yellow and green paper, a pen, cookies, and napkins*

Before the meeting, cut yellow and green paper into enough small slips for each person in the group to have one. On the yellow slips, write, "Hold this paper. Don't let anyone else see it. Do nothing special." On the green slips, write, "Congratulations! You're part of a special, select group. Find other people with green slips of

■ ■

paper, and congratulate them on their good fortune. Don't speak to anyone who doesn't have a green slip of paper." If you have a large group, you can write out the messages and then photocopy them onto yellow and green paper.

As kids come in, distribute the slips of paper randomly, and allow kids to mill about the room for several minutes. The kids with yellow slips represent the "outsiders"; the kids with green slips represent the "insiders."

Invite the group to gather around, but specify that those with green slips of paper should sit in the front, while the rest of the group should stand in back. Also hand out cookies to those with green slips, but ask kids to save them for later. Have a volunteer from the insiders read aloud Mark 2:15-17.

Then collect all the slips of paper, and have everyone sit in a circle. Ask:

● **Who were the insiders, and what was so special about them?**

● **Who were the outsiders, and what was wrong with them?**

● **How did it feel to be an outsider? an insider?**

● **In biblical times, there was a clear division between the insiders and outsiders. How are insiders and outsiders divided today?**

● **How did the Pharisees in the passage feel about including others?**

● **How did Jesus feel about it?**

● **Why did Jesus associate with "sinners"?**

● **What can we do to follow Jesus' example? What should we not do?**

Have each person who was an insider offer a cookie to an outsider and enjoy the treats together.

▪ Have Confidence ▪

PURPOSE: *to convey overcoming doubt and fear through a skit*

SCRIPTURE: *Matthew 14:22-33*

SUPPLIES: *Bibles and photocopies of the "Walking on Water" skit (p. 79)*

Following the skit, have volunteers read aloud Matthew 14:22-33. Ask:

■■

● How did Peter deal with his fears and doubts?

● In what area of your life do you face the most fears and doubts?

● How does God want us to overcome those feelings?

Close with a prayer, thanking God for his strength in dealing with our fears.

▪ Strings of Stress ▪

PURPOSE: *to help kids deal with stress*

SCRIPTURE: *Philippians 4:6-7*

SUPPLIES: *a Bible, ball of string or yarn, scissors, music, and a fun snack*

Have kids sit in a circle. Say: **Today we're going to talk about the stress in our lives. Let's pass around this ball of string. When it comes to you, name all of the stresses in your life that you can think of. For each stress you name, pull out about a foot of string. Once you've named all the stresses you can think of, cut off the string.** Start the string and scissors around the circle.

Once everyone has shared and has a length of string, have kids form trios. Select a person in each trio to be tied up first by his or her trio partners, using that person's string. (Be sure kids don't tie string around someone's neck.) Then the second person can be tied up by the third person in the trio. You can tie up the last person in each trio using his or her string.

(continued on p. 80)

Walking on Water

Scene: A teenager is preparing for a difficult dive at a school swim meet.
Props: You'll need a long, wide board.
Characters:
Tony, a teenage diver
Offstage Voice

Script

(Tony is standing on the end of a long, wide board, talking to himself as he looks at the "pool" in front of him.)

Tony: I don't know about this, God. *(Looks around as if surveying the crowd.)* If there weren't such a big crowd here, I'd climb down this ladder right away. *(Pauses.)* Maybe I should do that anyway. Yeah, that's it. I'll go back down. Coach will understand. He's probably seen it happen hundreds of times. *(Turns as if to climb back down, and then stops.)* No, I've got to do this. *(Confidently prepares to jump.)* Here I go—Tony Martin, diving maniac… *(He stops in midmotion)* What am I doing? That's a long way down. People have died falling out of chairs, and I climb ten meters to jump into a pool that feels like concrete if you hit it wrong. What am I, crazy? *(He starts to turn around as if to climb back down again, and then pauses.)* OK, OK…you're right, Lord. You have kept me safe every other time. Why should this be different? It's not like I have to walk on water or anything. *(He turns again as if preparing to dive, starts his diving motion, and is interrupted by the Offstage Voice.)*

Offstage Voice: The next diver is our current leader and last year's state champion: Tony Martin from West High.

(Tony is startled out of his self-talk and looks around the room.)

Tony: *(Smiles, waves to the imaginary crowd and walks confidently toward one end of the room. He's mumbling to himself as he walks.)* I hope they remembered to fill the pool… *(Freezes in midstep.)*

Once everyone is tied up, invite kids to a celebration across the room featuring music and treats. Turn on the music, and invite kids to join in the fun.

Stop the music. While kids are still tied up, ask:

● **How do you feel about being all tied up?**

● **How are the effects of the string similar to the effects of stress in your life?**

● **How does stress take away your sense of freedom?**

● **Is it possible to live so that stress doesn't have this effect on you? Why or why not?**

Read aloud Philippians 4:6-7. Ask:

● **Is it possible to not be stressed about anything as this passage suggests? Why or why not?**

● **According to this passage, what's the best way to deal with stress? Why is that hard to do?**

● **How can we help each other reduce the stress in our lives?**

Start the music again, and have kids work together to set each other free from the string. Turn the music down low, and ask kids to pile the string in the middle of their trio and pray together, asking God to show them ways to be stress reducers for each other this week. At the end of the meeting, let kids enjoy the snacks.

• Bag-o-Esteem •

PURPOSE: *to learn about accepting others*

SCRIPTURE: *Romans 15:1-7*

SUPPLIES: *Bibles, paper grocery bags, scissors, and markers*

Give teenagers paper grocery bags. Supply scissors, and have each person cut out holes for his or her eyes, nose, and mouth. Set out markers, and ask kids to write their names on their bags.

Choose volunteers to read aloud Romans 15:1-7. Ask the group to follow the Scripture reading carefully. Then have kids put the bags over their heads, walk around the room, and select words from the text to write on each other's bags. Kids might write words such as "endurance," "encouragement," "hope," "unity," and "accepted." After a few minutes, have kids remove their bags and read their Christian affirmations. Ask:

● **Why is acceptance and affirmation so important?**

■■

● Should the way we look influence whether or not we're accepted or encouraged? Why or why not?

Continue your meeting with a discussion about God's acceptance of us and our acceptance of others.

■ Clay Needs You ■

PURPOSE: *to explore ways to encourage others*

SCRIPTURE: *Hebrews 3:13*

SUPPLIES: *a Bible and a lump of clay*

Plan this opening around the theme of encouragement by using a fictitious character named Clay Thompson. Clay is represented by a lump of clay that you hold in your hand. Throughout the devotion, hold out the lump of clay for the group to see.

Say: **Clay is a talented guy. He plays in the band at his high school.** *(Roll the ball of clay in your hand.)* **He gets good grades and is popular with guys and girls. Recently his dad moved out of the house. Home became a sad and depressing place.** *(Pull off a little bit of clay, and hand it to someone.)*

After his dad left, Clay didn't feel like doing his homework. He'd just close the door to his room and listen to music. His grades started to drop. *(Pull off another piece of clay, and hand it to another person.)* **Clay didn't practice his saxophone, so when try-outs came, he moved down four chairs.** *(Pull off another piece of clay, and give it to a third person.)*

Clay's best friend, Seth, noticed something was wrong. "Hey, what's up, Clay?" he asked. "You're acting weird lately." Clay looked down and said, "Things are bad at home. My dad moved out." Seth simply mumbled, "That's too bad," and walked away. *(Pull off another piece of clay, and hand it to someone.)*

When Clay returned home from school that day, his mom was sitting on the front step waiting for him. "We need to talk, Clay," his mother said sadly. "Your father and I are getting a divorce." Clay was crushed. *(Flatten the lump of clay with your fist.)*

Stop the story, and choose a volunteer to read aloud Hebrews 3:13. Then ask the group to finish Clay's story with ways to build Clay back up again. Have people hand you their pieces of clay as they offer their encouraging suggestions. As the story unfolds, roll Clay back into a complete ball again.

After the story, give each person a small ball of clay. Have kids form groups of three, and have kids tell their group members about times they've felt like Clay. Each time someone offers an affirmation, have him or her give the encouraged person a piece of clay.

▪ Life's Not Fair! ▪

PURPOSE: *to read a creative interpretation that sheds light on success and evil*

SCRIPTURE: *Job 21:7-21*

SUPPLIES: *photocopies of the "Creative Reading for 'Life's Not Fair!'" handout (p. 83)*

Choose four readers, and give each one a script.
Reader 1—Job, who should stand apart from the other readers
Reader 2—a disgruntled teenage girl
Reader 3—a disgruntled athletic guy
Reader 4—a successful "wicked" person
After the reading, ask:
● **How does it feel when cheaters succeed?**
● **How can we deal with it when they do?**
● **What are wrong ways to deal with the success of wicked people?**
You can use this creative reading to open a discussion about Job's despair and ultimate victory.

▪ Love Wanted ▪

PURPOSE: *to discuss having a healthy respect for sex*

SCRIPTURE: *Philippians 1:9-11*

SUPPLIES: *a Bible, suitable "personal ads" from a newspaper*

Have kids form groups of four or less. Distribute ads from a newspaper "personals" or "dating" section. Have kids read through some of the ads. Then have kids discuss the following questions in their groups:
● **What do these people want?**
● **What are these people really looking for: love or sex?**

(continued on p. 84)

Creative Reading for "Life's Not Fair!"

Reader 1: "Why do the wicked live on?"

Reader 2: *(Incredulously)* She cheats and gets an A. I study and get a C minus!

Reader 3: *(As if in conversation)* ...steroids! So now he's starting this week while I sit on the bench.

Reader 4: Look, I'll just call in sick, and we'll go to the lake— like anyone will know.

Reader 1: "Their homes are safe and free from fear...They sing to the music of tambourine and harp."

Reader 3: I worked out all summer while he partied. So how come I'm the one on second string?

Reader 4: Let someone else pick up the slack at work. I need to work on my water skiing.

Reader 2: And she dates every night of the week! *(Sighs.)* Maybe I should lower my standards a little?

Reader 1: "[The wicked] spend their years in prosperity."

Reader 4: Hey, another promotion! And a raise!

Reader 2: *(Looks up toward heaven.)* It's just not fair!

Reader 3: *(Looks up toward heaven.)* It's just not fair!

Reader 1: "They say to God, 'Leave us alone! We have no desire to know your ways.' "

Reader 2: She used to be so close to you, God.

Reader 3: And then he makes jokes about me going to Bible study.

Reader 4: They need God as a crutch, and they act so self-righteous.

Reader 1: "Let [their] own eyes see [their] destruction; let [them] drink of the wrath of the Almighty."

(Readers 2 and 3 walk offstage. Reader 4 suddenly looks up, terrified.)

Reader 1: "When [their lives] come to an end."

Reader 4: *(Yelling)* No! It's not fair! *(Covers head with hands and freezes.)*

■■

● What's the difference?
● What kind of respect for sex do these people have?

Choose a volunteer to read aloud Philippians 1:9-11. Then say: **Today we're going to talk about sex respect. Sex respect is respect for the power of sex and for God's protective guidelines. We demonstrate healthy sex respect by the value we place on our bodies and how we conduct ourselves physically in relationships with others.**

▪ Doubt No More ▪

PURPOSE: *to understand God's power over doubts and fears*

SCRIPTURE: *Matthew 14:22-33*

SUPPLIES: *Bibles, newsprint, a marker, and tape*

Before the meeting, write on a sheet of newsprint, "Lord, we're afraid of (name of fear). Help us to trust you." On a second sheet of newsprint, write, "Take courage! It is I. Don't be afraid." Post both sheets in the front of the room.

Have kids form groups of no more than four, and have kids read Matthew 14:22-33 in their groups.

Say: **Peter had a hard time trusting Jesus because he was afraid. In your group, brainstorm for a list of situations in which you might be afraid. Be realistic. For example, it's not likely that you'll be thrown into a pit of vipers, but you could be teased because you refuse to drink alcohol at a party.**

Give kids several minutes to brainstorm, and then invite groups to share their situations.

Say: **Now choose one or more situations from your list that each person in your group can relate to.**

Write responses on the newsprint that says, "Lord, we're afraid of...Help us to trust you."

Then have groups take turns saying, "Lord, we're afraid of...Help us to trust you." Have kids finish the sentence with one of the situations written on the newsprint.

After a group reads a situation, have the rest of the kids respond by reading Jesus' words from Matthew 14:27b that are written on the second sheet of newsprint.

Have kids continue the activity until each group has had a chance to read at least one situation.

Lead kids in a Bible study about fear and ways to deal with it from a biblical perspective.

▪ Dealing With Authority ▪

PURPOSE: *to learn how to respond to people in authority*

SCRIPTURE: *Luke 20:20-26*

SUPPLIES: *a large pillow*

Before class, set up chairs in a circle.

Have kids sit in the chairs, and say: **Think of one person you respect. In a minute I'm going to ask each of you to tell about this person. But first I'd like to tell you a few new rules we have here today.**

First, there will be no whispering or talking out of turn.

Second, both feet must remain flat on the floor at all times. No exceptions.

Third, there will be no scratching, fixing hair, or movement of any kind.

To be sure everyone follows these rules, I'd like (name a group member) **to take this pillow and patrol our group.**

Give the pillow to the patroller, and say: **If you think the people here are out of line, go ahead and gently bop them with this pillow.**

Have kids repeat the rules, and start the sharing time. Teenagers can each tell about one person they respect and why they respect that person. Allow the pillow bopping to go on without interfering—even if there are complaints.

Continue for about five minutes, and then ask:

● **Who has the most authority in our group right now?**

● **Why do you think this person has authority?**

● **How are you feeling about this person right now?**

Retrieve the pillow, and then say: **We're going to talk about authority today and determine how we should respond to people who have it.**

▪ Yackety-Yak ▪

PURPOSE: *to perform a skit to understand the damage done by gossip*

SCRIPTURE: *Ephesians 4:29-32*

SUPPLIES: *a Bible, photocopies of "The Invitation" skit (p. 87) and props*

After kids perform the skit, read aloud Ephesians 4:29-32. Ask:

● **Why is it so easy to get caught up in gossip?**

● **According to Ephesians 4:29-32, what are good examples of how we should talk about others?**

Use this skit as an opener to a discussion on the temptation to gossip and how to overcome that temptation.

▪ Strength in Numbers ▪

PURPOSE: *to play a learning game to examine the temptation of sexual sin*

SCRIPTURE: *1 Thessalonians 4:1-8*

SUPPLIES: *Bibles, paper, and pencils*

Choose one guy and one girl. Have kids form a tight circle around the girl. If your group is large, form smaller circles of eight to ten people, each surrounding a female volunteer. Have the male volunteer stand outside the circle and try to break through to tag the female. Allow the male volunteer several tries before having him switch roles with the girl. Then ask:

● **How did it feel to try to tag the person in the circle?**

● **How did it feel to be in the center of the circle?**

(continued on p. 88)

The Invitation

Scene: Kids are eating in a high school cafeteria.

Props: You'll need trays, paper plates, forks, cups, books or backpacks, a table, and chairs.

Characters:

Teresa

Kris

Stacey

Paula

Script

(Teresa and Kris are sitting in the cafeteria, eating lunch. Stacey enters, talking to Paula.)

Stacey: And this is the ever-dangerous cafeteria. Oh, Teresa, Kris, this is my cousin, Paula Stevenson. She's visiting for a week, and they're letting her go to classes with me today.

Teresa: Nice to meet you, Paula. Too bad they had to be serving Tuna Surprise on the day you're visiting—not a very nice first impression!

Paula: *(Laughs.)* That's OK. We have Tuna Surprise back home, too. Actually, everyone's been really nice.

Stacey: Oh, I invited Paula to Bible study on Thursday night. I thought she could probably meet a lot of new people there.

Kris: Well, she'll meet a lot of people there, all right. People like Jennifer Thomas and Cathy Ivers—they're so stuck up! They only go to Bible study to talk about how many guys they've gone out with!

Teresa: Or to show off their new clothes. I'm so sick of them! And they're always flirting with that jerk, Mark Andrews. You know, I heard he got some girl pregnant over at Washington High.

Stacey: Hey, I heard that too. Only I thought it was at Central...or was it Westview? Anyway, if Jennifer or Cathy ever go out with him, I wouldn't be surprised if it happened again. I heard that Cathy went to the mountains with some college guy.

Kris: Yeah, but you know, there *are* some really nice people at Bible study. Like Marissa and Kelly. I mean, they're pretty nice...even if Kelly does have really bad breath. Did you ever notice that? I sat next to her last week, and it was gross. And she totally sings off-key, too.

Paula: Hmm...that sounds like a really...um...interesting Bible study.

Teresa: Yeah, it's a great place to meet people.

■ ■

● How does this game illustrate the difficulty of remaining sexually pure?

● What do you think the wall of people represents?

Have kids form groups of three. Give each group a Bible, paper, and a pencil. Ask groups to read 1 Thessalonians 4:1-8 and then rewrite the passage as though they were writing a letter to their school friends.

When groups are finished, have them read their letters aloud. Then ask:

● Why should people avoid sexual sin?

● Why does it matter so much to God?

● If a person has had sex already, what does this passage say to him or her?

● How can we help each other stay sexually pure?

Lead kids in prayer, thanking God for his help and grace for purity.

▪ Changing Commands ▪

PURPOSE: *to explore ways to handle change in their lives*

SCRIPTURE: *James 1:16-18*

SUPPLIES: *a Bible*

Open the meeting by giving kids a variety of instructions. Change your mind several times while forming groups in preparation for an "activity." Act indecisively about the best group formation for the activity. Pause to let kids move after each instruction. For example, you might say, "Standing an arm's length apart, form a large circle and face outward. Well, uh, no—let's just get into two parallel lines and face each other. Maybe...instead...find a partner. Um, let's just form a circle."

After you've given your final instruction, ask:

● What was it like having to adjust to all my changing instructions?

● How is that like the way you feel when you deal with change in your life?

● What is the toughest thing about change?

● When is change exciting or exhilarating? exasperating or exhausting?

Have a volunteer read aloud James 1:16-18. Then say: **In the** midst of change, God does not change. Let's discuss how God can help us adapt to the changes in our lives.

▪ School Crazed ▪

PURPOSE: *to play a hectic game that leads into a discussion on school stresses*

SCRIPTURE: *Matthew 6:34*

SUPPLIES: *a Bible and school supplies*

Before your meeting, gather a variety of school supplies such as pens, pencils, rulers, books, notebooks, and folders.

Have kids sit in chairs in a circle. Hand a person one of the school supplies. On "go," have kids pass the item clockwise around the circle. Call out, "Faster, faster!" to encourage kids to speed up the action.

Continue adding items until all school supplies are being passed around. When someone drops an item, stop the action and have the person pick up the item. Restart the game, and continue until someone else drops an item. Keep adding school supplies until you have far too many for kids to handle. Then stop the game, and congratulate the group. Ask:

● **How did you feel as the game became more hectic?**

● **How is that like the way school becomes sometimes?**

● **What advice might Jesus give you to handle school pressures?**

Read aloud Matthew 6:34. Ask:

● **Why do you think Jesus encourages us not to worry about tomorrow?**

● **What are some practical ways we can keep ourselves from being overwhelmed by school?**

Continue the meeting with Bible study, discussion, and prayer to offer kids new insights in dealing with school pressures.

▪ Thankless Job ▪

PURPOSE: *to try to relate to their parents' feelings*

SCRIPTURE: *Psalm 127*

SUPPLIES: *newspaper and tape*

■ ■

Have kids form pairs, and give one partner in each pair some newspaper and tape. Tell pairs that they're to build the tallest creation they can with the supplies they have. But partners can't speak to each other. One partner must hold the supplies, and the other partner must do all the building. The partner holding the supplies may dispense only one item at a time to the partner who's building.

Give pairs three minutes to complete their creations. Congratulate the winners. Ask the partners who held the supplies the following question:

● **How did it feel just to hold the supplies without being allowed to build or talk?**

Ask the partners who did the building the following question:

● **How did it feel to be dependent on your partner but not to say any words of appreciation to him or her?**

Say: **Sometimes parents feel the same emotions that the partners who held the supplies felt. Parents want to be involved in and give input about our lives, but they're seldom appreciated for what they do. During this meeting, we'll talk about how we can better understand and appreciate our parents.**

Special-Occasion Openings

"Today in the town of David a Savior has been
born to you; he is Christ the Lord."
LUKE 2:11

*T*eenagers look forward to special occasions because they offer variety from the usual routine. Holidays bring parties, treats, gifts, and excitement to kids' lives. So liven up your youth meetings, and take the opportunity to teach lessons connected to these special days.

▪ Tie the Knot ▪

PURPOSE: *to learn how to handle dating relationships in a way that honors God*

SCRIPTURE: *Romans 13:8 and Hebrews 13:1*

SUPPLIES: *a Bible*

On Valentine's Day try a new twist on a well-known game. Have kids form a circle and join hands. Then challenge kids to create a knot with their hands and bodies—without letting go of each other's hands. Encourage kids to crawl over, under, or around each other at random—whatever it takes to become as tangled as possible.

Once everyone is super-tangled together, ask:
● **What was fun about getting all tangled like this?**
● **How is a dating relationship like this knot we've created?**
Have kids untangle themselves without releasing each other's hands. Ask:
● **Was it hard to untangle yourselves without letting go of each other? Why or why not?**
● **How is untangling our knot like breaking up with a boyfriend or girlfriend?**
Read aloud Romans 13:8 and Hebrews 13:1. Ask:
● **What's the best way to handle a breakup? What's the worst way to handle it?**
● **What can we learn from these Scriptures and our knots to help us handle our dating relationships in a way that honors God?**

▪ How Far Would You Go? ▪

PURPOSE: *to explore commitment to friends through a Good Friday study*

SCRIPTURE: *Romans 5:9-11*

SUPPLIES: *a Bible, masking tape, and toy cars*

Before the meeting, use masking tape to mark off ten equal distances on the floor.

Give each person a toy car, and have kids put their cars behind the first line on the floor. Instruct kids to move their cars to the next line for each of the following acts of friendship they would normally do. Say: **Move your car forward one line if you would typically**

- talk to a friend on the phone during the week.
- greet a friend in the hall at school.
- share your lunch with a friend who forgot his or her lunch.
- give a friend money when asked.
- let a friend stay at your house when he or she is in trouble.
- stick up for a friend in front of other friends.
- confront a friend when he or she is doing something harmful.
- confront a friend when he or she is doing something illegal.
- take the blame for a friend in trouble with the law.
- give a friend your most prized possession to pay his or her debt.

After the kids have moved their toy cars, ask:

- **How far do you think friendship should go?**
- **What does a person gain by showing strong commitment to another person?**
- **How do you feel when a friend asks you to do something that goes beyond your present level of friendship?**

Ask a volunteer to read aloud Romans 5:9-11. Then say: **While we were God's enemies, he made a way for us to be his friends. Let's talk about that more.**

▪ Easter Light ▪

PURPOSE: *to follow a maze in the dark to experience what the disciples might have felt like*

SCRIPTURE: *John 16:16-22*

SUPPLIES: *a Bible, sheets, a flashlight, and a plate of treats*

In a large room, set up a maze with chairs and tables covered with sheets. Make sure your maze has different paths to follow. Set a plate of treats at the end of the maze. Set up a flashlight on its end to shine on the ceiling.

Gather everyone at the start of the maze. Then say: **On "go," I want each of you to get down on your hands and knees and crawl through this maze. There will be a reward for those of you who reach the end.**

■■

Turn on the flashlight, turn off the lights, then say: **Go!** When everyone has finished the maze and discovered the treats, turn on the lights, and ask:

● **How did it feel to be in the maze?**

● **How would you have felt if there had been no light at all to follow?**

● **Did you depend on someone else to guide you or did you try to find your own way?**

Ask volunteers to read aloud John 16:16-22. Ask:

● **How do you think the disciples felt when Jesus died?**

● **Why did they have trouble understanding what God's "big-picture plan" was for Jesus?**

● **How was the disciples' experience like going through this maze?**

● **What was the "light" they had to guide them through those dark days?**

Have kids form groups of three. Ask group members to share a time they couldn't find any "light" to follow in life or a time when they had a hard time believing God could be in charge of the big picture.

▪ There She Is... ▪

PURPOSE: *to think about and discuss appreciating their moms*

SCRIPTURE: *Deuteronomy 5:16*

SUPPLIES: *a Bible, index cards, pencils, and paper "sashes" for contestants to wear*

Have kids form teams of no more than four. Explain that each team must choose one of its members to compete in a contest—don't tell them what the contest is yet.

After each contestant is chosen, tell groups that the contest is for the "Perfect Mom." Hand each contestant a paper sash to wear. Then give groups pencils and index cards to write responses for their contestants to the following questions:

● **What do you like best about your kids?**

● **If you had an entire day to yourself, what would you do?**

● **What's the hardest thing about being a mom?**

Give teams a few minutes to coach their contestants. Then

interview each "mom" using the three questions listed above. When the interviews are completed, have kids applaud all of the moms.

Ask a volunteer to read aloud Deuteronomy 5:16, then ask:

● **What do you think would make someone the perfect mom?**
● **How realistic were the moms you created?**
● **What does the word "honor" mean to you?**
● **What is our responsibility toward our mothers?**

Have kids end the activity with sentence prayers of thankfulness for those who care for them.

▪ Lunch-Box Treats ▪

PURPOSE: *to make cookies and discover the importance of listening to God*

SCRIPTURE: *Job 42:1-2 and Jeremiah 29:11-13*

SUPPLIES: *Bibles, blindfolds, rope, copies of a cookie recipe, cookie ingredients, utensils, and an oven*

Have an adult volunteer help you prepare for this opening. For every two people, you'll need one blindfold, one piece of rope, a copy of the cookie recipe, cookie ingredients, and utensils.

Have kids form pairs. Have one partner be the "guidance counselor" and one partner be the "student." Blindfold the students, and tie the counselors' hands behind their backs. Place each pair in front of its cookie recipe, ingredients, and utensils.

Say: **Now that you're back in school, it's important that you all have a cookie-making lesson. Each counselor-student pair gets to practice making cookies. The recipe, ingredients, and utensils are in front of you. Students, no peeking. You must listen to counselors' instructions to prepare the cookies. Counselors, no touching. You can only tell the students how to make the cookies.**

After the cookies are mixed and placed on cookie sheets, help pairs take off their blindfolds and ropes. Ask the following questions while the cookies bake:

● **What was fun or frustrating in your role as a student? as a counselor?**
● **Students, what would have happened if you hadn't listened to your counselor?**
● **In life, who is it important to listen to?**

Ask volunteers to read aloud Job 42:1-2 and Jeremiah 29:11-13. Ask:

● **What do these verses say about listening to God?**

● **Why do we try to do things our own way without God's guidance?**

Say: **God is always with us. If we listen and obey him, he will guide us every day of our lives.**

Ask a volunteer to close in prayer, thanking God for his guidance.

▪ Scare Me! ▪

PURPOSE: *to have some scary fun and then learn what Scripture says about the reality of evil in the world*

SCRIPTURE: *Matthew 4:1-11; Romans 12:9; and 3 John 11*

SUPPLIES: *Bibles and anything you need to play a scary trick*

Before your meeting, prepare a scary trick to spring on the kids. For example, you might have someone surprise the group by jumping out of a box. Or you might have someone turn out the lights unexpectedly.

Have kids form groups of no more than five. Encourage groups to come up with fun, safe, creative ways to scare someone. Allow no more than five minutes for groups to brainstorm for their ideas.

Then ask groups to explain their scary ideas. While the last group is explaining its idea, implement your scary plan to startle kids. When kids calm down, ask:

● **What was it like to be surprised or scared?**

● **Why do people like to scare each other?**

Say: **We can scare each other in silly, fun ways. But the devil is real, and evil is real. Let's see what the Bible says about that.**

Begin your study using these passages: Matthew 4:1-11; Romans 12:9; and 3 John 11.

▪ Yummy Gifts ▪

PURPOSE: *to help kids explore what it means to be thankful*

SCRIPTURE: *Matthew 7:11-12; 2 Corinthians 9:10-15; and James 1:17*

SUPPLIES: *Bibles, group members' favorite snack foods*

■■

Before the meeting, find out what your kids' favorite snack foods are. Then buy something small for each group member based on what you discover—a small bag of pretzels or peanuts or a miniature candy bar, for example. If you can't find out about a group member's favorite food, choose something he or she probably will like, such as a can of soda pop.

When kids arrive, have them form groups of no more than four. Ask groups to read 2 Corinthians 9:10-15 and spend a few minutes in prayer, thanking God for all the good things in their lives. Then gather kids together, and distribute your food gifts while telling kids how thankful you are that they're a part of the group.

Have each person find someone who has a different food and pair up with that person. Ask pairs to discuss the following questions:

● **What was it like to receive a gift you weren't expecting?**
● **Were you thankful to receive this gift? Why or why not?**
● **How is the way you responded when you got this gift like the way you respond when others do nice things for you?**

Continue your meeting by asking kids to share further insights they have regarding this Scripture. In addition, you may want to have kids study Matthew 7:11-12 and James 1:17, which are about God's gifts.

▪ Just Like Christmas ▪

PURPOSE: *to affirm each other at Christmastime*

SCRIPTURE: *1 Corinthians 12:4-7*

SUPPLIES: *a Bible and Christmas decorations for the meeting room*

Gather kids together during the Christmas season for a special affirmation time. If possible, meet in a home that's decked out for the holidays, or decorate your meeting room for Christmas.

Have kids form a circle, and ask a volunteer to sit in the center of the circle. Have group members tell the person in the center of the circle some positive reasons he or she is like a particular Christmas item. For example, someone might say, "Jerry, you're like the lights on the tree because you have such a colorful and cheery personality."

Allow each person to spend one minute in the center of the

circle, and then have that person trade places with someone new. Continue until each person has sat in the center of the circle.

Ask a volunteer to read aloud 1 Corinthians 12:4-7. Remind kids that we are all gifts from God to one another.

• God's Gift •

PURPOSE: *to affirm each other with the giving of "gifts"*

SCRIPTURE: *Matthew 2:9-11 and John 3:16*

SUPPLIES: *Bibles, construction paper, markers, and pencils*

Have everyone sit together in a circle. Tell group members to think of what gifts they'd like to give each person in the group, regardless of price. Encourage kids to choose personal gifts based on their friends' interests and needs. For example, someone might give a friend a scholarship for college, a CD of his or her favorite music, or a giant chocolate bar. Tell kids the sky's the limit, but no unkind gifts are allowed.

Give each person a sheet of construction paper, a marker, and a pencil. Tell group members to decorate their papers to look like gift boxes and to write their names at the top with the markers. Then have kids pass their "boxes" to the right.

Say: **When you get a new box, read the name at the top, write down the gift you would like to give that person, and sign your name next to the gift idea. Continue passing the boxes until everyone has his or her own box back.**

Allow time for kids to read their boxes silently, and then let volunteers read aloud their gift lists. Ask the gift-givers to tell why they chose particular gifts for their friends.

Ask for volunteers to read aloud Matthew 2:9-11 and John 3:16. Encourage kids to discuss the eternal gift that God gave—his own Son.

• Dashing Through the Snow •

PURPOSE: *to play a fun game for the holidays*

SCRIPTURE: *none*

SUPPLIES: *two winter hats, two strings of jingle bells, two wagons, confetti, and "Jingle Bells" music*

■■

Open a Christmas party or meeting with this fun game. Set up a simple course with four chairs set at the corners of a 15×30-foot rectangle. Scatter confetti "snow" on the course.

Have kids form two teams. Each team starts the race with "one horse" pulling the "open sleigh" wagon with a rider inside. Have the riders put on the winter hats for the sleigh ride; the horses must carry or put on the strings of jingle-bells. Anything goes as long as the riders stay in their sleighs and the horses stay on the course.

When the first pair completes the course, the horse becomes the rider in the sleigh and the next person in line becomes the horse, and the previous rider goes to the end of the line. Have kids continue this rotation until the first rider becomes the last horse.

While kids are dashing, play the song "Jingle Bells." Oh, what fun!

▪ A Promised Savior ▪

PURPOSE: *to focus on the promise of Jesus' birth*

SCRIPTURE: *Matthew 1:18-23*

SUPPLIES: *a Bible, scissors, a photocopy of the "Creative Reading–A Promised Savior" handout (p. 100), a bowl of apples, candles, and matches*

Ask five people to volunteer to read the parts from the creative reading, and give each volunteer one section from the handout. Have kids sit in a circle, with the lighted candles and the bowl of apples in the center. Dim the lights, and ask the readers to begin.

Following the creative reading, suggest that students take the apples home and eat them—with thanksgiving—as reminders of what God has done for them through his Son, the Lord Jesus.

▪ Bunches of Memories ▪

PURPOSE: *to explore the value of common memories and give thanks for the group's experiences during the past year*

SCRIPTURE: *Psalm 78:1-7*

SUPPLIES: *Bibles, newsprint, a marker, and several bunches of grapes*

(continued on p. 101)

Creative Reading—
A Promised Savior

Directions: Photocopy and cut apart this handout for use during the creative reading.

✂ ─

Reader 1: Christians in the early church performed dramas to teach people the stories of the Bible. These became known as "miracle" and "mystery" plays.

The "paradise play" portrayed the creation and sin of Adam and Eve and their expulsion from the garden of Eden. Since this play often concluded with the promise of the coming Savior, it was performed around Christmastime. A tree decorated with apples was used to symbolize the garden of Eden. Christians began to set up this "paradise tree" in their homes on December 24, the feast day of Adam and Eve.

✂ ─

Reader 2: You are invited to take an apple, a symbol for the first sin of human beings. Look at it, and think of sins or things in your life that you wish to turn away from. *(Pass the bowl of apples around the circle.)*

✂ ─

Reader 3: *(Read aloud Matthew 1:18-23.)*

✂ ─

Reader 4: The promise of Jesus' birth, spoken through an angel of the Lord, reminds us that we aren't trapped by sin; we have a Savior, Jesus. One of the names for Jesus is Immanuel, which means "God with us." God is with us and loves us. He will help us turn away from the things we do wrong and guide us in the best direction for our lives. Let's use this opportunity to be quiet and listen for God's direction. *(Bow your head.)*

✂ ─

Reader 5: *(Allow a few minutes of silence before speaking.)* Let's pray: Dear God, we thank you for the birth of your Son, Immanuel. We celebrate your presence with us. We know that your love will give us the power we need to turn away from the things in our lives that hurt us. And you can turn us toward all that is good and helpful for our growth. In Jesus' name, amen.

■ ■

Ahead of time, write on newsprint the three following questions:

1. Would you rather remember
   A. a big family reunion,
   B. a quiet meal with close relatives, or
   C. a special time with two or three friends?

2. Would you rather remember
   A. a meal with lots of great food,
   B. a meal with fun company, or
   C. a meal with entertainment?

3. Would you rather remember
   A. a long trip to see family,
   B. a short trip to be with friends and family, or
   C. a time of preparing your home for guests?

Post the questions so the group can see them. Also post three signs—"A," "B," and "C"—in three corners of the room.

Gather kids around. Tell them that you'll read aloud three questions and that they are to move to different corners of the room depending on their answers. Read aloud the three questions, giving kids time to run from one corner to the next.

After all the questions, ask: **Which of these experiences would make you feel the most thankful? Explain.**

Have kids with similar responses form groups. (If your group is small, form one group.) Ask a volunteer in each group to read aloud Psalm 78:1-7.

Pass around the grapes, and tell everyone to take some but to wait to eat them. After everyone has a handful of grapes, have each person share a positive memory of a special occasion that happened during the last year and then eat a grape.

When a person has only one more grape, ask him or her to share something special that's happened in the youth group during the year—something that will be remembered for years to come.

Just-for-Fun Openings

"This is the day the Lord has made;
let us rejoice and be glad in it."
PSALM 118:24

*H*ave some fun with your teenagers with these openings. Encourage them to laugh, let off steam, share amusing memories, and just be silly during these creative activities.

• Musical Grab Bag •

PURPOSE: *to grab an accessory item for laughter and fun*

SUPPLIES: *a grocery sack, a variety of costume accessories, lively music, and a camera (optional)*

Before the meeting, fill a grocery sack with a variety of costume accessories such as old ties, slippers, crazy glasses, strange hats, jewelry, pantyhose, eyebrow pencils, shower caps, and artificial flowers.

Ask kids to sit in a circle. Start the music, and have kids pass the bag until you stop the music. Ask the person left "holding the bag" to reach in without looking and put on whatever he or she pulls out. As the bag is passed around the circle, kids will continue to don more accessories and create outlandish outfits.

This is a great photo opportunity!

• Comedy Hour •

PURPOSE: *to make each other laugh*

SUPPLIES: *none*

For some good old-fashioned fun, have kids form pairs, and ask each partner to complete any three of the following sentences:

● The funniest television commercial I've seen this year is...

● The most needlessly repeated phrase a parent or teacher ever used with me is...

● The best clean joke I've heard recently is...

● The funniest person I've ever met is...

● The funniest face I've ever seen someone make is... (Have kids attempt to create the faces for their partners.)

● The best practical joke I've heard of is...

▪ Birthday Mixer ▪

PURPOSE: *to let off steam while forming groups*

SUPPLIES: *newsprint and a marker*

Before the meeting, copy the following statements in large letters on a sheet of newsprint.

January—Shout, "Get out there and shovel!"

February—Whisper nervously, "I think someone likes me."

March—Whiningly say, "When is Easter vacation?"

April—Say confidently, "Chocolate bunnies give you zits, you know."

May—Say, "Only thirty more days to go, and then I'm outta here."

June—Say, "Mom, can I borrow the car?"

July—Say, "Dad, the pastor needs the money for the youth rally!"

August—Say solemnly, "School is starting—bummer!"

September—Excitedly say, "Oh! Who's the new girl (boy)?"

October—Shout, "Boo! Look, he jumped!"

November—Say, "I ate too much turkey!"

December—Say, "Mom and Dad, I just want a car."

On "go," have kids each begin saying the line from their birthday month. For example, kids who have birthdays in November would say, "I ate too much turkey!" at the same time kids who have birthdays in July say, "Dad, the pastor needs the money for the youth rally!"

Have kids form a group with the people who are saying the same line. Each group can work together during Bible study, discussion, and further activities.

▪ Win, Lose, or Mold ▪

PURPOSE: *to have fun molding biblical themes from clay*

SUPPLIES: *index cards, a pen, and modeling clay*

On separate index cards, write biblical characters, themes, or items such as "Noah's ark," "David and Goliath," "the serpent," "the manger," "the empty tomb," and "Jonah and the big fish."

Have kids form two teams. Give each team a large lump of clay. Explain to kids that they will participate in a sculpting contest based on biblical characters and themes.

Place the cards face down between the two teams. Have a person on each team choose a card and mold the clay into a shape to help his or her teammates guess the topic. Instruct the molders not to give any verbal clues. In addition, molders cannot write letters or numbers in the clay.

Have teammates take turns sculpting and guessing the topics.

• Scar Show 'n' Tell •

PURPOSE: *to meet each other and talk about scars*

SUPPLIES: *none*

Gather everyone in a circle. Ask kids to each say their name, then show and tell how they received one of their scars! They must be able to show the scar to talk about it. Kids love telling their personal "war stories," and they're a riot to listen to. Each student who doesn't have a scar to show can tell about a "scar to my pride"—a funny mistake or most embarrassing moment.

• Find Ralph •

PURPOSE: *to relive some great memories through photos and a fun game*

SUPPLIES: *photos of your youth group, scissors, a bulletin board, glue, a marker, and supplies to create background scenes as described below*

Before this activity, gather copies of photos you've taken of your youth group over a long period of time. Cut around each young person in the pictures. On a bulletin board, create a background scene such as a beach, a school class, or a church auditorium. Glue the pictures of the young people to this background scene, overlapping them to create a huge collage.

Then post a list of things to find in the collage. For example, write, "Find Karen tying her shoe," "Find Bill eating a hot dog," or "Find three people wearing hats."

Your youth group members will enjoy this opening activity, and it'll get them ready for fun learning to come.

• Masterpiece in a Minute •

PURPOSE: *to test creativity in a wild way*

SUPPLIES: *finger paints, aprons or trash bags, paper, and a box of facial tissue*

Give each teenager three different colors of finger paint, an apron or trash bag to protect clothing, and a sheet of paper. Then have each "artist" create a "masterpiece" in one minute using only his or her nose to apply the paint. For a variation, blindfold the artists!

Have the group vote on the best painting, and award the artist an extra-large box of Kleenex tissues.

• Graffiti Wall •

PURPOSE: *to creatively let off steam*

SUPPLIES: *butcher paper or newsprint, tape, markers, and crayons*

Open a special event, party, or meeting by giving kids the opportunity to create a graffiti wall in the meeting room or gym. Before the event, cover the walls with white butcher paper or newsprint. Then set kids loose with markers and crayons to decorate the paper with art, words, Scripture texts—anything appropriate that they feel moved to do.

Use this opener to draw new kids into your meetings, to decorate for a specific theme, or to highlight a big event.

• Rush Hour •

PURPOSE: *to expend some energy before settling down for the meeting*

SUPPLIES: *none*

Have kids number off. (The last person's number will equal the total number of kids in your group.) Then have kids arrange their chairs in two straight lines that face each other with an open space down the middle. Choose one person to be the "traffic cop," and have him or her stand between the lines of chairs. Remove the traffic cop's chair from the line.

Tell the traffic cop to call out three or more numbers. The people with those numbers must exchange seats. Tell the traffic cop that he or she must try to sit down as well. Whoever is left standing then becomes the new traffic cop.

For added fun, the traffic cop can occasionally yell, "Rush hour!" Then everyone has to try to exchange seats with the person sitting across from him or her while the traffic cop tries to sit down.

■ Rice Sculptures ■

PURPOSE: *to create a sculpture for fun or as a tie-in to your meeting theme*

SUPPLIES: *overcooked rice, plastic utensils, and plastic tablecloths or garbage bags*

No matter what climate you live in, you can provide gooey hands-on fun to winter's outdoor art form—ice sculpting. Have teams create sculptures from sticky, overcooked rice using their hands and plastic utensils. Be sure to protect the working surfaces with plastic tablecloths or garbage bags.

Give kids free creative rein to sculpt whatever they wish, or assign a subject that ties in with your topic for the meeting.

■ Up-Tempo Musical Chairs ■

PURPOSE: *to get the wiggles out before the study begins*

SUPPLIES: *music*

Add variation to Musical Chairs by placing chairs randomly throughout a large room. When the music starts, kids will run from chair to chair and not be tempted to "camp out" by a single chair. After the music stops and the person left standing is eliminated, remove one, two, or three chairs. When only three people are left in the game, make sure the remaining chairs are the ones farthest apart!

To add even more challenge to the game, spread chairs throughout adjoining classrooms, making sure the music can be heard in all areas.

• "Joust" for Fun •

PURPOSE: *to learn each other's names in a high-energy game*

SUPPLIES: *two baseball caps, two foam-rubber bats, two foam playground balls, and two pairs of sunglasses*

Say: **The word "joust" comes from the days of the knights in shining armor. It's a competition between lance-bearing, horseback-riding knights. Today we'll joust with some different equipment—baseball caps for helmets, foam-rubber bats for lances, and playground balls held between the knees as your horses. You'll wear sunglasses to protect your eyes.**

Have kids form two teams. Ask kids to line up side by side, facing the opposing team, ten to fifteen feet apart. Form an equipment pile at one end of the line for each team. Include in each pile a baseball cap, a foam bat, a playground ball, and a pair of sunglasses.

Say: **I'm going to give everyone a number. I'm not going to count you off in sequence. This way, no one on the opposing team will know who he or she will compete against in the game.**

Whisper a number in each player's ear. Count off one team: one, two, three, four, and so on. Count off the other team in random order: three, seven, four, and so on.

Say: **When I call a number, the players who have been assigned that number will each "prepare to joust" by rushing to their team's equipment, putting on their baseball cap (helmet), placing the ball between their knees (horse), putting on their sunglasses (eye protection), grabbing hold of the foam bat (lance). Then each player will try to knock the baseball cap off the other player's head first. As you joust, your team will cheer you on by yelling your name again and again.**

Continue the jousting competition until all numbers have been called and everyone has had the chance to play and learn each other's names. If you use this activity with a group that's well acquainted, use it to open a discussion on encouraging one another.

• Swarm Tag •

PURPOSE: *to have fun in a high-energy game*

SUPPLIES: *none*

For this game, you'll need twelve or more players and a large field or open area.

Form at least three groups of four to ten players. Tell each group to choose one player to be "It." On your signal, have each group play a game of Tag. Whenever a group member is tagged, he or she becomes "It" for that group and must call out, "I'm 'It'!"

Here's the catch: All of the groups must play in the same area. In addition, if someone who is "It" tags a member of another group, the two players switch groups, and the person who was tagged becomes "It" for his or her new group.

This game will turn into chaos after a short while, but that's part of the fun.

· White Water ·

PURPOSE: *to form a "wave" of fun*

SUPPLIES: *shoes*

Have kids form two teams of equal size. Have one person from each team sit on the ground with his or her legs together and straight out. Then have another person from each team sit next to the first, but facing the opposite direction. Each person's ankles should touch his or her neighbor's hips. Have kids continue to form lines in this back-and-forth fashion until both teams have created long lines. Then have members of each team grab hands with the people next to them to form a continuous "wave."

Balance a shoe on one end of each team's wave, and then tell the teams to pass the shoe to the other end. Instruct team members not

to use their hands to move the shoe. Kids will be able to move the shoe by leaning close to each other and moving their arms up and down and left and right. If the shoe falls, the team must place it at the beginning and start again. Have teams race each other to see which shoe can "ride the rapids" most quickly.

Tip: On a hot day, use a hose to douse kids with water as they move a water balloon down the rapids.

▪ Play It Again ▪

PURPOSE: *to praise God with creative music*

SUPPLIES: *slips of paper, a pen, and lively music*

Before your meeting, write the names of six to eight musical instruments on separate slips of paper. You'll need enough slips for each person to have one.

Tell kids it's their chance to be in a lively jazz band. Give them each a slip of paper, and have them practice making their instrument sounds. Then have kids each practice "playing" a well-known tune such as "When the Saints Go Marching In."

Play the lively music you brought, and have kids walk around and trade slips with different people. When the music stops, have each person play the new instrument and find others who have the same instrument. Once their group is formed, have kids play the tune using their new instruments.

Then start the music, and have kids trade slips again while the music plays. This time when you stop the music, call out "Mixed band!" Have kids form groups with a variety of instruments and play the song again.

Scripture Index

5613